Great Art Sales
of the Century

John Parker

Great Art Sales of the Century

Pitman Publishing/London
Watson-Guptill Publications/New York

First published in Great Britain 1975 by Pitman Publishing Ltd,
39 Parker Street, Kingsway, London WC2B 5PB

Published in the United States 1975 by Watson-Guptill Publications,
a division of Billboard Publications, Inc., One Astor Plaza,
New York. N.Y. 10036

Library of Congress Cataloging in Publication Data
    Parker, John, 1926—   Great art sales of the century.
    Includes index.
    1. Art auctions—History   I. Title
N8602.P37   380.1'45'7   75-5852

U.S. ISBN 0–8230–2150–5
U.K. ISBN 0 273 00385 2

Filmset by V. Siviter Smith, Birmingham.
Printed in Great Britain by Unwin Brothers Ltd
The Gresham Press, Old Woking, Surrey, England.
A member of the Staples Printing Group.
Colour printing by W & J Mackay Ltd, Lordswood,
Chatham, Kent.

G2:11

Acknowledgements

The connoisseur of art and the fine arts market will find little that is new to him in this book, which is designed more for the everyday lover of beauty than for the expert. But the author wishes to acknowledge his debt to those upon whose expertise he has so freely drawn, particularly the authors of *Art at Auction* and Christie's *Reviews of the Year*; and especially to Susan Rose and John Herbert of Christie's, and Susan Redhead and Stanley Clarke at Sotheby's. Thanks are also due to Christie's and Sotheby's for making the illustrations available. There is one cautionary note: figures described as 'records' may well have been exceeded since the time of writing, as inflation and a growing scarcity of great works have their effect.

Contents

54 black and white plates.

26 colour plates:

    1–18 appear between pages 24 and 25;

    19–26 appear between pages 72 and 73.

1. Christie's, St James's, London.

Introduction

When the idea of *Great Art Sales of the Century* took shape, I thought it might not be a bad thing to start from the grass roots, as it were. It may be dramatic to sit (too close together, slightly sticky) in the great auction room of Christie's or Sotheby's in London and watch a major work of art sold for a million pounds; but everything that is bought and sold by auction is second hand. It has been used by someone or other at some time or other. It has been looked at, sat on, slept in, read, eaten off or with, or maybe just parked on the mantlepiece and dusted once a week for a hundred years. When you sell a possession, so my romantic reasoning went, you're not selling an 'objet d'art' or even of 'vertu', you're selling a bit of your life, the sort of stuff that dreams are made on.

The name of Sir Everard Radcliffe, Bt., though no doubt famous throughout Yorkshire, has rung few bells outside that noble county, and when I learned from Christie's that Rudding Park, his great home, was for sale 'lock, stock and barrel' I was unmoved. I mean, it wasn't as if the Devonshires were to sell up Chatsworth. But I was assured that the sale was going to be a typical one, so I decided that my quest would start at Harrogate.

Rudding Park is a genuinely beautiful estate three or four miles outside that gracious old spa, but at first sight the big house was a disappointment. Apart from the fact that its double-bowed façade was badly in need of a coat of paint and inside it smelt of damp, it had all been packed and parcelled up ready for the sale. It had exactly the same forlorn air that any ordinary house has on moving day, only more so. Beside the house, on the close-clipped grass, a huge marquee had been put up. This was where the sale was to be held, and row upon row of uncomfortable wooden chairs borrowed from the village hall had been set out to accommodate the locals, as well as the scores of dealers from London and overseas who were expected to attend. It was October, and to alleviate the nip in the air, portable gas cylinders had been brought in for the heaters strung round the poles of the marquee. I hoped they weren't as dangerous as they looked. Some of the larger items of furniture—bureaux, commodes, chests of drawers and tables in every form of material from marble to mahogany—were laid out round the sides of the tent, and facing the audience from the left front was a copy of Christie's famous rostrum, designed by Chippendale himself.

In fact the sale, which lasted for two days, was great fun indeed. Everyone seemed to enjoy themselves, including two ladies in real fighting form who bid up the price of a perfectly nauseating picture of a child, by a fortunately unknown painter, from its notional value of £50 to 700 guineas. For me, there were two particularly memorable moments.

The first came when a pair of old, plain, oblong but very big settees, covered in stained and tattered yellow rep, were put up for sale. My dealer friend, sitting next to me, had marked down in his catalogue £140 with a question mark against the Lot, and indeed all the professionals dropped out of the bidding thereabouts. But a sort of madness swept through the tent, and when the gavel banged down its finality the price was £1,400. The dealers broke into spontaneous applause.

The Chairman of Christie's, Mr I. O. (but known as Peter) Chance, came down to conduct part of the sale. He is an imposing, urbane figure, and I was surprised to see that he seemed to be slightly ill at ease; not with the sale, that is, but in some physical discomfort. He kept brushing his hand across his head as if something was irritating him.

The movement was catching. Soon the man in front of me was doing the same thing, and the woman next to him. I was doing it myself. My scalp felt itchy. I looked around the tent, and scores of people were scratching their heads and necks. I passed my hand

2. The magic of the saleroom—at Sotheby's.

across my head again and looked at it. There was the answer. The heat from the gas fires and the press of people had brought up from the grass, of all things, hundreds upon hundreds of tiny *money-spiders*. They were obviously in the right place. Sir Everard Radcliffe's goods and chattels, right down to and including the kitchen sink, fetched £170,000—and the *good* pictures had been sent for sale to London, and the *best* silver to Geneva.

Before I launch into the main business of this book, which is to tell some of the stories of, and behind, the great sales of the century, it's probably a good idea to outline the history of art auction sales and the growth of the two remarkable firms who have been almost exclusively responsible for building a world-wide business with a turn-over of over £100 million a year. A very large proportion of this business is based in London.

Both Sotheby's and Christie's were founded in the mid-eighteenth century, as an indirect result of the Industrial Revolution which brought great wealth to Britain as a whole and unprecedented pros-perity to new sections of British society. It is an historical fact that when any country becomes rich, one of the first things it wants to do is spend. So, in the eighteenth century the Grand Tour became the fashion, and the people who went on it brought back vast numbers of French, Dutch and Italian paintings, silver, furniture and other works of art from all over the continent. Wealth and the vast expansion of trade which brought about the British Empire of the seventeenth and eighteenth centuries sent traders, politicians, administrators—and armies—to the four corners of the earth. The terror which followed the French Revolution ended the reign of Paris as the cultural and artistic centre of Europe; dozens of dealers fled to London and settled there in the same way as the Huguenot silversmiths had escaped from the religious persecution of other years. London became the great depository for the plunder of civilizations from each of the five con-tinents.

Art and literary auctions themselves were originated by the Dutch, and were actually introduced into England in 1676. In fact the early sales were nearly always of books, and it was in 1744 that one Samuel Baker, of Russell Street, Covent Garden, held the first of a continuous series of sales which made him the first professional book auctioneer. (Twenty years later, when Christie's began, there were more than sixty auctioneers in London.)

At first the business moved slowly. The total turnover in 1744 was only £826, and it was not until 1767 that Baker was joined by a partner, George Leigh. Quite soon afterwards he retired to 'a delightful villa which he built at Woodford Bridge, near Chigwell, in Essex.' His portrait, by Grignion, which hangs in Sotheby's offices, shows a sedate but determined old man in a white bob-wig and plum-coloured coat. His gavel (celebrated in verse as 'this sceptre of dominion which now decks the courteous hand of Leigh') was retired only a few years ago, after two centuries of service, to the status of an exhibit.

In the year of Baker's death his nephew, John Sotheby, joined Leigh in partnership. He was the first of three generations of Sotheby's who between them carried on the firm for nearly a hundred years and who made its name internationally famous in the fine art world. He incidentally laid down the pronunciation which so many still seem to find difficult—Soth (the 'o' as in 'love') er-bee.

In 1861 the last of the Sotheby's died, leaving his name behind him and the firm in charge of one John Wilkinson. Wilkinson was joined three years later by Edward Grose Hodge, whose son, Tom Hodge, was left as sole partner in 1909, the point from which the modern history of Sotheby's was launched—by chance.

Hodge was a sportsman, and on joining a new shooting syndicate he found as a fellow-member a rising ecclesiastical lawyer, Montagu Barlow, who combined a keen eye for business with a scholarly and antiquarian taste. Hodge, who had no successor in his own family and frankly didn't seem interested, was prepared to sell the business. Barlow, seeing the possibilities, found two friends with similar vision and tastes, and Sotheby's passed into the hands of an unlikely group. Of the new partners, Barlow secured a seat in Parliament in 1910, entered the Cabinet as Minister of Labour in 1922 and retired from Sotheby's in 1928. Geoffrey Hobson became known as a versatile scholar, author of a number of works and the world's leading expert on bookbindings. He died suddenly in 1949. Felix Warre, after serving as President of Oxford University Boat Club, and obtaining his apprenticeship in the arts while in business in the Far East, successfully controlled the finances of Sotheby's for nearly forty years.

When the 1909 syndicate took over, they had the book world at their feet. For at least two generations almost every British library of importance that had come on to the market had passed through their hands. They had attracted many foreign consignments, such as the libraries of Talleyrand, of Napoleon, and of Jerome Bonaparte, King of Holland (consigned by his nephew, afterwards Napoleon III). Moreover, they had awaiting sale three consignments of superb quality (and bulk) which eventually realized over five million dollars in the auction room: the Britwell library, whose sale is still the world's greatest; the Huth library and the Phillips collection, the last of which has still to be sold at the time of writing.

But they wanted to branch out; so in 1917 Sotheby's moved to the eighteenth-century building in New Bond Street which is still their headquarters and expanded into fine art sales in the widest field. On a modest scale, they were no strangers in the wider market. They had long been specialists in porcelain, glass, coins and engravings and classical and Egyptian antiquities, and during the heyday of so-called 'Academy' art had sold a fair proportion of contemporary

4. Sotheby's, New Bond Street, London.

paintings. But they had never previously been housed or equipped for the great art sales; and though in 1917 expansion was to be expected, even the brightest dreams of the proprietors did not foresee that within forty years the firm's turnover would increase twentyfold and its book sales—although still predominant in their own field—would soon account for no more than ten per cent of the business. Or that in 1958 Sotheby's would stage what was *the* Sale of the Century, when seven Impressionist paintings fetched nearly £800,000, firmly re-establishing London as the centre of the world art market, a position it has consolidated and strengthened ever since. But more of that later. Let's first have a look at Sotheby's two-centuries-old rival—Christie's. Or, to give the firm its full title, Christie, Manson and Woods.

5. James Christie—a former midshipman.

James Christie was born in Perth in 1730. He became a midshipman
in the Royal Navy, but resigned his commission before he was twenty.
He then became a junior partner to an auctioneer in Covent Garden
(could it have been that same Samuel Baker?) and at the age of
thirty-six announced his intention to set up on his own in rooms
in Pall Mall. It was a much more flamboyant start to business life
than that of Sotheby's, for Christie had style, a silver tongue and
influential and generous friends. David Garrick, the actor, lent him
£5,000 (a very large sum in those days) and on 5 December 1766,
he was able to hold his first sale in rooms 'mechanically constructed
under the immediate direction of some of the finest artists in the
kingdom'. Gainsborough was his next-door neighbour, and they

became great friends. The artist painted Christie's portrait on condition that it was hung in a prominent position in the saleroom.

Christie would take anything for sale—pictures, silver, furniture and household effects—warming pans, boxes of tallow candles, loads of 'truly excellent meadow-hay' from a farm not two miles from St James's Palace. On another day, in two successive lots, there was a barrel-organ and a coffin. The latter, as was urbanely described by James, had been prepared for a citizen who had made a 'most remarkable recovery from a malady usually regarded by the medical confraternity as fatal.'

'Let me entreat you, Ladies and Gentlemen, permit me to put this inestimable piece of elegance under your protection. Only observe the inexhaustible munificence of your superlatively candid generosity must harmonize with the refulgent brilliancy of this little jewel. Will Your Ladyship therefore do me the honour to say £50,000? A mere trifle, a brilliant of the first water, an unheard-of price for such a Lot, surely?'

It was with tongue-twisters like that that James Christie began each sale. Even in those days he became known to the cartoonists as 'the Specious Orator'. But he got away with it. He was very good-looking, had a commanding presence, persuasive charm and got on well with everyone. Gainsborough and other artists like Sir Joshua Reynolds played a great part in his life. In those days it was the fashion for the aristocracy and the very rich to have their portraits painted, but as there were no exhibition rooms James Christie 'allowed' artists to hang their paintings in his saleroom. In this way he came to know many of the famous in the land and made many other valuable contacts. Thus, when the latter wanted to sell their property, they naturally came to Christie's. By the turn of the century, Christie's was included in a contemporary reference book, *Microcosm of London*, and was one of the capital's chief institutions.

One of Christie's first coups came about through the French Revolution. The famous courtesan, Madame du Barry, paid a secret visit to London after the fury had passed, to seek James Christie's help in selling her collection of jewels. Word of her intentions leaked out and on returning to France she was betrayed by a servant. She was duly arraigned before a Tribunal, charged with stealing and selling treasures of the State, and beheaded in 1793.

All London came to Christie's auction rooms fourteen months later to see what is described in the catalogue as 'a Most Capital and Superb Assemblage of Valuable Jewels of Most Singular Excellence, Beauty and Perfection, late the property of Madame La Comtesse du Barry deceased.' They realized just under £10,000.

The sale that was perhaps the climax of James Christie's career never even passed through the auction rooms. This was the sale of

THE SPECIOUS ORATOR.

WILL YOUR LADYSHIP DO ME THE HONOR TO SAY £50-000

—A MERE TRIFLE.—A BRILLIANT of the FIRST WATER.

an unheard of price for such a lot, surely.

6. A cartoon, dated 1794, of *The Specious Orator*.

superb Old Masters in the Houghton Collection which were sold to Catherine the Great by George Walpole, grandson of the Prime Minister, on the basis of a valuation by James Christie.

Then there was the spirited engagement between Nelson and Christie when the former midshipman (rtd) came under fire from the Admiral. Christie had obtained for sale the collection of Sir William Hamilton, and among the paintings was a portrait by Vigée Le Brun of Nelson's beloved Emma. From his flagship *St George* he wrote to Emma on

10 March 1801: 'But you are at auction—Good God, my blood boils.' In the next letter, having failed to have the picture withdrawn, he wrote: 'How can any man sell your resemblance; to buy it many would fly. As for the original, no price is equal to her merits. Those of her dear mind and heart if possible exceed her beauty.'

He finally bought it for 300 guineas. 'If it had cost me three hundred drops of blood,' he told Emma, 'I would have done it with pleasure.' These two letters today hang proudly in Christie's boardroom.

If the eighteenth was the century of the Grand Tour, then the nineteenth was surely the century not only of massive new wealth in the United States but also of a considerable redistribution of fortunes in Britain. Dotted throughout this century at Christie's were sales from the greatest houses in the land, of the Dukes of Buckingham and Hamilton, Buccleuch and Somerset, of the Earl of Dudley and the Marquess of Exeter, the Duchess of Montrose, of the Lords Lonsdale and Leighton. It is no exaggeration to say that it was these picture sales at Christie's in the late eighteenth and nineteenth centuries that were, in many ways, the basis of the modern collections in museums from Berlin to Boston, from Tokyo and Sydney to Paris and Leningrad.

Another facet of Christie's work was the disposal of pictures from the studios of famous artists. Thomas Gainsborough, Christie's friend over so many years, was the first, setting a precedent that has been followed ever since by a whole string of similar events; studio sales of Reynolds, Landseer, Raeburn, Rossetti, Burne-Jones, and Sargent, right up to the two sales in the 1960s of the Augustus John studio,

7. Part of one of Admiral Lord Nelson's letters to Lady Hamilton. This letter is now in Christie's Boardroom.

which together realized £133,000.

In 1803 James Christie died and was succeeded by his son. Twenty years later the firm moved to its present premises in King Street, London, leaving them only for a short while when it was blitzed in 1940.

Since the French Revolution, London has always been an important art centre, for many reasons which are strengthening as the years go by. It has always been an important centre of communications, particularly so in these days of easy air travel, and the experience gained by the dealers over the last 200 years has made the London market far more professional than those of many other countries. One seemingly accidental but important factor has been that because of the strength of the turnover and the demand for works of art, London salerooms have been—and are still—able to sell at the lowest commission in the world—down to ten per cent; there are no customs duties in Britain on any works of art over 100 years old, nor sales taxes on them as in most other countries.

Aided by these factors, the art boom which started in the mid-1950s was sparked off by the penal taxation in post-war Britain, which brought many superb works on to the market. Post-war recovery elsewhere and the general rise in the standards of living in many parts of the world brought about the market demand. Prices have increased still further as the result of laws in America which make works of art tax deductible if donated to museums or universities (making it very difficult if not impossible for British institutions to compete).

Finally the flight of confidence from the world currencies of the late 'sixties and 'seventies has driven many people to invest their money, not in stocks and shares or building societies, but in works of art that—so far—show little sign of doing anything but increase enormously in value. The money-spiders have been spinning hard in the past few years.

Art sales boom—or art inflation, whichever you like to call it. Sometimes one gets the impression when reading the newspapers or talking to the *cognoscenti* that the only thing that matters is the money. True, there's a fascination of its own in the spectacle of a million pounds or more being spent in two minutes flat for some old oils daubed on canvas. But that's not all that the sales are about. They're about people, about living human beings and the things they have lived with and loved. Go round the salerooms at any time—they're still among the best free exhibitions when there isn't a sale being held—and you'll see what I mean. More than two-thirds of the thousands of items sold by Sotheby's and Christie's in London or Parke–Bernet in New York each year fetch less than £100 each. Sales are about the little old lady's teapot: is it worth £10 or £10,000? They're about avarice, and courage, about gambling and skulduggery and the irresistible urge to strike a better bargain than one's neighbour.

CATALOGUE
OF
PORCELAIN,
PLATE,
Decorative Objects and Furniture,
THE PROPERTY OF THE LATE
ANDREW W. McKAY, ESQ.
(Sold by Order of the Executors);

ALSO

Japanese Carvings in Ivory and Wood,
Lacquer, Bronzes, and other Objects of Oriental Art;
Old English and Oriental Porcelain;
Embroideries, Decorative Objects and Furniture,
FROM VARIOUS SOURCES;

AND A SMALL COLLECTION OF
EUROPEAN ARMS AND ARMOUR,
Of the 16th, 17th and 18th Centuries,
THE PROPERTY OF A LADY:

WHICH
Will be Sold by Auction by
MESSRS. CHRISTIE, MANSON & WOODS,
AT THEIR GREAT ROOMS,
8 KING STREET, ST. JAMES'S SQUARE,
On THURSDAY, JANUARY 11, 1900,
AT ONE O'CLOCK PRECISELY.

May be viewed Two Days preceding, and Catalogues had, at
Messrs. CHRISTIE, MANSON and WOODS' Offices, 8 *King Street*,
St. James's Square, S.W.

8. Catalogue of the first sale of the century.

9. The K'ang Hsi blue and white ginger jar (Prunus vase) which sold for 5,000 guineas in 1912.

The Red Cross Fund

The very first sale of the twentieth century took place, as far as one can discover from the records, at Messrs Christie, Manson and Woods' premises in King Street, St James's Square, London, West 1, on 11 January 1900.

It wasn't a record breaker. The porcelain, plate, decorative objects and furniture, the property of the late Andrew McKay, Esq., and

Japanese Carvings in Ivory and Wood,
Lacquer, Bronzes, and other Objects of Oriental Art;
Old English and Oriental Porcelain;
Embroideries, Decorative Objects and Furniture,
from various sources;

and a small collection of
European Arms and Armour,
of the 16th, 17th and 18th Centuries,
the property of a Lady.

to quote the catalogue, sold for the munificent sum of £438.16s.6d.

One wonders, though, whether in the 1970s one would pay only £8.18s.6d. for 'An old Worcester and Crown Derby tea and coffee service, fluted and painted with flowers, foliage and ribands in blue and gold. . .' or £38 for 'a suit of mail, cased in purple velvet, embroidered with gold galon, consisting of haubeck and chausse, hemispherical helmet, the border damascened with gold, camail attached and a pair of hinged vambraces similarly decorated with embroidered velvet gauntlets', for which, for some reason or other, the Marquis of Dalhousie had found no use.

At this time, Sotheby's were still concentrating mainly on the sales of books (none the less prosperously for that, according to the records) and it wasn't until towards the end of the First World War that they began the major expansion which would embrace the whole of the art world. Christie's plugged on successfully, however, selling one collection of French snuff boxes and objets d'art in 1904 for the incredible sum of £344,000; and in 1905 an assortment from the Huth collection (Sotheby's were disposing of the great Huth library) for £17,000. It included a Prunus vase for 5,000 guineas that had been picked up in Wardour Street for 12s.6d.

The First World War, which brought tragedy to so many millions, nearly brought Christie's to its knees for the first and only time in two centuries. The confident predictions in 1914 that the war would be over in a few months proved unfounded, and Christie's, in common with the whole spectrum of British life, found itself drained of its able-bodied men, its business in ribbons and not a work of art in sight. The firm was on the verge of being closed down when, out of the national necessity, a use was found for the business as a valuable ally of the Red Cross Fund.

The Joint Committee of the Red Cross Society and the Order of St John of Jerusalem was issuing urgent appeals for subscriptions and many people who could not send money were contributing jewels and gifts in kind of every sort. How to dispose of these became a mounting problem, until the Art Correspondent of *The Daily Telegraph*, A. C. R. Carter, suggested calling in Christie's, who at once obliged by giving their services and those of their staff free to the cause. This was no mean gift indeed, for the ravages of the war reduced the staff to the two elderly directors, Mr Lance Hannen and Mr W. B. Anderson who, with occasional help from a couple of girls, collected, organized, classified and catalogued and sold thousands upon thousands of items in a whole series of Red Cross Sales stretching from 1915 to 1918.

The first results were disappointing, even though King George V and Queen Mary headed the list of donors. In the class-conscious society of the day this was some cachet, but even so Christie's were forced to postpone the sale from February until April. By 30 March the catalogue was ready—with 1867 lots spread over 351 pages. The sale opened on 12 April and continued for twelve days with a break for the weekend, ending on 27 April. Suddenly the idea took fire. On the third day, two Irish potato rings belonging to a young airman, Samuel Pepys Cockerell, who had been killed in Egypt, were sold as an offering by his parents and bought by a peer, Lord Newlands, who promptly returned them to the donors in memory of their son. Lord Newlands put up a Stradivarius violin, which Lady Wernher bought for £2,500 and gave it back to be put up the second time, whereupon it fetched another £1,400. The artist John Singer Sargent, who had abandoned portrait painting, was persuaded to do 'just one more' as a donation. At the auction Christie's obtained a 'blind' offer of £10,000 for this portrait, but, when the donor himself died in the sinking of the *Lusitania*, the question of the sitter had not been decided. His executors commissioned Sargent to paint a portrait of President Woodrow Wilson of the United States; and sent in their cheque.

The sale made nearly £38,000 for the Red Cross, and it was decided to do it all over again the next year. Christie's, however, found that their own business had unexpectedly revived (thousands of pounds were being made in the most unexpected quarters due to the war, and the sale of art treasures picked up as suddenly as it had fallen away). So the Red Cross decided to collect the goods themselves and hold and catalogue them in a special building, leaving Christie's merely to conduct the auction. The contemporary account describes the problem with some irony.

'In addition to the Press appeal, a number of sub-committees were appointed to deal with different classes of goods, having as chairmen experts or amateurs who could help in influencing and valuing gifts. An elaborate system of enumeration was adopted in order to prevent confusion in identifying the donors and these classified lists, together with thirty filing cases of correspondence, were handed over to Christie's when the time came, as an aid to dealing with the immense quantity of material suddenly unloaded upon their premises.

'But the trouble did not end there. Christie's felt compelled to overhaul the index for themselves, and to see whether important gifts or people had been overlooked, and vice versa. Such mishaps would arise, say, over the following articles:

2416 Lady Glitterham, a diamond tiara.
3750 Miss Smith, a cup and saucer.

'The tiara cannot be traced, and a feverish search is set up at the depot. Finally it is unearthed and turns out to be a paste bangle. The second entry has passed unnoticed until a member of the china sub-committee happens to ask: "What do you think of the Sèvres Ecuelle?" Another search is instituted and Miss Smith's cup and saucer prove to be the Ecuelle and the printers have to be instructed to enter a fresh lot before going to press.'

The most ticklish business of all perhaps was the task of correcting the donors' names, printed over every lot. People are notoriously careless about their signatures, and even about their sex, and Christie's catalogue staff made use of every directory and book of reference that was available in checking the names. But nothing could avail to prevent the arrival of indignant letters and callers the day after the catalogue was issued, when such expressions as 'gross carelessness', 'any schoolboy' and 'absurd ignorance' were freely banded about, for the most abounding generosity sometimes goes hand in hand with an irritable sensitivity over trivial if unavoidable mistakes.

The 1916 sale lasted fifteen days, and was an improvement on the first, as the public had grasped the idea that if they really wanted to swell the fund, they had to send in items which other people cared to buy, not just rubbish they could get rid of. A Major-General gave a collection of Dr Johnson's letters, which are now in the British Museum; Lady Wernher outdid her first-year performance by buying a fine Toft dish for 650 guineas, putting it up for auction again and buying it herself a second time for 600 guineas. Then she presented it to the British Museum. The total for the fifteen days was £64,000.

And so it went on. In 1917 the total was over £71,000; in 1918 it was £150,000; and the total for the four sales was well over £300,000.

But that was not all. One idea of the Red Cross Committee was to ask for pearls to be made into a necklace, during the 1918 sale, and the response was sufficient for two necklaces, which sold for £2,000. Encouraged, the Red Cross formed a special committee headed by Princess Victoria the Princess Royal, to collect pearls for a giant Red Cross necklace, the proceeds to go to the sick and the wounded. The appeal was advertised all over the world, and more than 4,000 pearls flooded in. It was decided to split them into several necklaces, which rather nullified the original idea, but enlarged the proceeds. An exhibition of the pearls was held at the Grafton Galleries, and at first it was the intention to hold a gigantic tombola, or lottery. This suggestion stirred up any amount of outcry from the anti-gamblers and, although Lord Lansdowne tried to introduce a short Act legalizing lotteries in the case of war charities, the Archbishop of Canterbury managed to prevent its being passed. After this triumphant vindication of the powers of virtue, the lottery project fell through, and the jewels were handed to Christie's who sold them (with some benevolent help from the big dealers of the day) for £84,000. Finally, Christie's staged a Gold and Silver sale which cleared over £53,000, bringing an aggregate of nearly £½ million for the Red Cross and the Order of the Hospital of St John from the seven sales.

10. Sir Max Beerbohm's cartoon of Christie's, drawn for the highest bidder at one of the famous 'Red Cross Sales' held during the First World War for charity.

The 'Twenties
The Holford Sales

The man who fathered the Red Cross sales, A. C. R. Carter, was one of the great characters in British journalism in the first half of the twentieth century; an imposing if somewhat formidable figure who graced the auction scene with his illuminating presence and accounts in *The Daily Telegraph* for more than forty years. In 1928 he was asked to contribute to Christie's first *Review of the Year*, a task he performed (as no doubt he did everything else) with diligence and a leisurely style inherited from a more gracious era. His subject— the great Holford sales which were the major events of the 'twenties— kept him and his readers occupied through twenty pages, but the rolling phrases could not obscure an acute and perceptive mind.

In 1928, then, he wrote:

'When I survey the remarkable events in the season of 1927–28 I begin to wonder what will be the expanded dimensions of Christie's art sales in 1968. My own experience as a watcher and a chronicler of very great dispersal during the past forty years has caused me to cease from marvelling at auction results; and it has certainly fortified me in the determination to refrain from imposing any limitation on the acquisitive appetites of collectors who continue to spring up and multiply in every rich state of the civilized world.

'The futility of any attempts at prophecy can be illustrated in a flash. When I had to write about the picture sales of 1888, the first Blockow sale had happened and, strange as it may seem today, the highest prices of the year were 5,500 guineas for Rosa Bonheur's *Denizens of the Highlands* and 4,900 guineas for Landseer's *Braemar*. Another Bonheur picture brought 4,200 guineas; the famous *North-West Passage*, by Millais, 4,000 guineas; Müller's *Lycia*, 3,750 guineas and, as Sir Joshua's delightful *Mrs Payne Gallwey and Son* had realized 4,100 guineas in the Gatton Hall sale, the chief six pictures of the year at Christie's totalled 26,450 guineas. Although this surprised many people, I am now relieved to find that I contented myself by describing the occurrence as "unusual".

'Yet few of the habitués of Christie's rooms in 1888 could then look forward to a sale in 1928 when the chief six pictures would amass a total of 198,000 guineas. All the six appeared in the Holford dispersal last May, headed by a Rembrandt at 48,000 guineas, and by a second Rembrandt at 44,000 guineas; the third place being filled by the Van Dyck *Abbé Scaglia*, which irresistibly attracted Sir William Ewert Berry to Christie's and caused him to bid in person until he had won the prize at 30,000 guineas.'

In passing, it is interesting to note what happened in 1968, the year to which Carter was looking forward. Christie's sales totalled £7,241,636 ($20,276,480), over half of it in pictures. Van Gogh's *Portrait of Mademoiselle Ravoux* fetched 150,000 guineas, a record at the time for the artist and Stubbs' *Goldfinder* (colour plate 19) made 72,000 guineas ($211,680).

Carter, like many latter-day journalists, couldn't help dropping a name or two:

'. . . To visit Christie's has always been held as a necessary part of a liberal education, and every man desirous of adding to his knowledge of the arts and humanities never ceases to treat Christie's as a post-graduate course of self-instruction in first-eye observation. In my day I have seen every famous or cultured man as a visitor at some time or another, especially prominent statesmen and distinguished men of affairs.

'At one sale, for example, I remember seeing Mr Asquith, as he then was, sitting by the side of his future bride, Miss Margaret Tennant, while Lord Rosebery and Mr Arthur Balfour looked on. Again, too, when Lord Curzon's collection was sold at the beginning of the 1927–28 season under review, I recalled several occasions when I had espied him marching in measured steps around the West Room, obviously reciting under his breath the speech which he had prepared for delivery in the House of Lords later in the day. Lord Lansdowne was another eminent statesman who would examine the pictures on view in the large gallery and then retreat to the quieter West Room to rehearse an address in the true "solvitur ambulando" manner counselled by the ancients. As for living statesmen, I have got them "on the list" in the words of Gilbert's Koko.'

Carter was there at the Holford sales. He tells how Robert Stayner Holford, a Victorian businessman, started his collection in 1843 by paying the then handsome price of 6,000 guineas for *thirteen* selected pictures from the collection of Sir Thomas Baring, the banker. Yet *one* of these, the Van Dyck *Abbé Scaglia*, made 30,000 guineas, and the Murillo *Girl with a Veil* fetched 5,600 guineas. Holford paid 700 guineas in 1849 for Rembrandt's *Maurits Huygenns* and that realized 10,000 guineas at the sale; another Rembrandt, *Marten Looten* which had cost Holford £700 went for 26,000 guineas; and so on.

The first Holford sale in 1927 made £156,000; and on 17 May

in the next year £364,000 established a day's total which stayed for a long time as a record; the following day a mere £52,000 changed hands. The overall total, £572,000, established a collection record, and old Joe Duveen (Sir Joseph, later Lord) lost a bet that it would not reach half a million pounds.

11.   A great picture sale at Christie's, 1888.
From an engraving published in *The Graphic*.

12. Portrait study for *Madame Gautreau*, by John Singer Sargent. Now in the Tate Gallery, London.

The 'Twenties
John Singer Sargent

The brilliant water colours of John Singer Sargent, R.A. made a fitting decoration for the high summer of 1925 when his whole studio came up for auction by order of his trustees. In the centre of the right-hand wall of the great saleroom was the large unfinished *Portrait of Madame Gautreau*, surrounded by other pictures. Hundreds of visitors, among them many Americans, thronged the saleroom for days before the sale itself, forecasting confidently that this or that picture would fetch £400 or so. But all forecasts were well below the mark. The first forty lots made over £30,000 and wiped out all previous records for the sale of modern paintings.

The total for the first day was £146,000 for 162 lots, although the *Madame Gautreau* was withdrawn; it had been bought privately by Sir Joseph Duveen for the extension wing he was building for the Tate Gallery on Millbank, London. Another portrait, of *Claude Monet painting the edge of a Wood* was also withdrawn. The auctioneer, Mr Lance Hannen, announced that it was being presented to the same gallery by two sisters, who watched the sale.

The contemporary account says that there was evident throughout the sale a sort of Sargent hunger 'only to be accounted for by the rarity of the occasions on which the artist's work could be picked up in a saleroom, and his reluctance during his lifetime to part with drawings that he did for his own pleasure in his later years'.

Sargent himself was a modest man, and frequently exhibited his lesser works as 'not for sale', leaving some discretion to the gallery. On one occasion, a visitor wanted a Sargent sketch, marked 'not for sale' and inquired with the management if it could be bought, and if so, what the price might be.

The management suggested £100, but the purchaser would not go beyond £60. With some trepidation, the manager approached the artist with the offer. Sargent replied: 'If the deal has gone through let it stand. But the drawing is not worth so much.'

The second day's sale was nearly as remarkable, with some high prices being paid for Sargent's studies from the Old Masters, principally Velasquez. One copy of the head of Balthazar Carlos, which started bidding at 50 guineas, was eventually knocked down for £1,680. The total for Sargent's pictures was over £182,000 (over $500,000 at the current exchange rate) which, in the 1920s, was a major triumph.

The American Scene

The American auction scene with its plush interiors and superbly lighted galleries is, compared with its British counterpart, a relatively young creation. Certainly its respectability dates back less than 100 years to the 1880s, when a pint-sized auctioneer with a sharp little goatee beard and button-black eyes formed the firm of Thomas E. Kirby and Company to sell off surplus stocks accumulated by the American Art Gallery, easily the most sumptuous commercial art gallery in New York and run by Richard F. Sutton and an art dealer named Rufus E. Moore.

Moore and Sutton, perhaps because of their grandiose ideas, failed to prosper, and in 1883 Kirby joined Sutton to run the newly-formed American Art Association (AAA) to promote American art. It didn't do very well, but it had luxuriously appointed premises in Madison Square, and became something of an American institution (that didn't take very long in the 1880s!). Kirby took a trip abroad, ostensibly because of ailing health, and studied the great London auction houses. He didn't like the system of secret reserve prices the European auctioneers had instituted to protect themselves from 'Ring' buying; he didn't like the 'Ring' either, but nor did he have any time for the freebooting American auctions of the time, with their fake buyers, fake sellers, and fake pictures.

In 1885 the AAA was given the chance to run its first auction of art treasures collected by the president of the Metropolitan Bank who had speculated unwisely and too well in railways that went broke. Sutton objected strongly to any hint that the AAA was a saleroom, but Kirby coined the word 'managers' to appease him, and the sale went ahead. It fetched $405,000. It was an amazing sum for those days and it put the AAA on its feet. Two years later Kirby sold the accumulated paintings and objets d'art of Mary Jane Morgan, the widow of Charles Morgan, a nearly illiterate owner of coastal sailing vessels who became the biggest shipowner in the United States. She had pinched and scraped and managed for her tyrant husband for twenty years, and when he died she took to shopping for beauty with her reticule stuffed with thousand-dollar notes. Her collection made up the first million-dollar sale, and it was not matched for more than twenty years, although Kirby and the AAA prospered mightily on lesser sums in the meantime.

America's first great sale of the twentieth century began on 5 April 1910. Charles T. Yerkes was an archetypal product of the booming Americas of the 'seventies and 'eighties. Never was there such an unloved, corrupt, brash, self-made, stinking-rich tycoon. By the time he reached twenty-four he had his own banking and brokerage house in Philadelphia; by thirty he was married with two children; by thirty-five he was in jail, sentenced to two years and nine months for embezzlement. Thanks to the efforts of his wife, he was out in seven months and within a year he had his fortune back. He became the streetcar mogul of Philadelphia and then Chicago; his ambitions growing with his fortune, he moved overseas and was one of the founders of London's vast underground system (although he found British public servants less gullible and less corruptible than those of America). He was a glutton for everything—money, mansions, mistresses and the works of great and lesser Masters. For above everything he craved beauty; and when he died in 1905 he left behind a collection of the world's most beautiful mistresses, another of incomparable Eastern carpets the like of which hasn't been seen since and yet another of paintings. He also left an illusory fortune or two, most of which was swallowed up by his creditors and by legal wrangles. Eventually, his picture collection came under Kirby's hammer.

Like Yerkes and his misdemeanours, the sale was something larger than life. Kirby had to contend with heavy opposition from the lawyers, who wanted to accept an offer from the British art dealer, Lord Duveen (the great one himself) of $1,250,000 for the contents of the whole of the Yerkes mansion in New York; then he braced himself for a concerted effort by the 'Ring'; and lastly he had to fight off an attempt to stop the auction by Yerkes' creditors. But in spite of everything the sale went ahead, and proved to be, as Kirby said it would, the dawn of a new era in art sales in America.

The newspaper *The Sun* reported on its front page that no such art sale had taken place before in America. 'Records fell about Mr Kirby like glasses swept from a table . . . the dollars seemed to be rolling along the floor from the gallery of the hall like water flowing from a Croton tap. . .'

Several records went before Joseph Turner's *Rockets and Blue Lights* came up for auction. It was known that Yerkes had paid about $78,000 for the painting and had kept it in his London office for prestige purposes; but Turner was virtually unknown in America. Kirby started the bidding at $50,000 and there was hardly a murmur throughout the hall until Duveen won the contest at $129,000—by far and away the biggest price paid for a painting in the United States. Twenty-four hours later, Frans Hals' *Portrait of a Woman* went to the American dealer Knoedler, after a spirited battle with Duveen, for $137,000 . . . and when the sale was totted up at the end of the day, taking into account $281,000 for the rugs (a fraction of what Yerkes had paid for them) and some handsome prices for the mansion furnishings, Kirby was able to announce a total of $2,200,000—nearly a million more than Duveen's original blanket offer.

Kirby and the AAA reigned supreme for twenty-five years, but in 1911 they felt for the first time the cold winds of competition. It came from the AAC—The Anderson Auction Company—and in the dusty world of books. The AAC had been founded by John Anderson, a quiet book auctioneer who had done well without any spectacular success. Early in the century he had 'discovered' a young man called Arthur Swann managing a tiny booksellers in Liverpool, and in 1902 Swann crossed the Atlantic to join him. Swann had ambitions well beyond those of Anderson, and when Anderson sold the AAC to an astute businessman called Major Emory S. Turner he got his chance. Thanks to the patronage of the multi-millionaire bibliophile Henry E. Huntington, of railway fame, Swann and the AAC prospered, and in 1911 snatched the book plum of the century from under the nose of Kirby and the AAA.

It was the library of Robert Hoe, the man who made his fortune with the rotary printing press. His hobby over the years had been book collecting. His house on New York's 36th Street was packed with thousands upon thousands of rare volumes—a Roman Missal presented in 1420 to Henry V of England by Charles VI of France; the first printed editions of Homer and Euclid, examples of Caxton's presses, the first printed edition of the *Canterbury Tales* and many more. He could choose from fifty different versions of the *Compleat Angler*.

The library nearly went to the AAA, for Kirby's reputation was at its height, but Swann, in a moment of sheer genius, recalled an article of studied vituperation that had once attended one of Kirby's book sales. He dug it out and Major Turner persuaded the Hoe executors that Kirby, although a great seller of paintings, would get things bookish all wrong. Swann's ruse worked; and he proceeded to make good his rival boast by producing a catalogue of such generous and intricate detail that it ran to 750 pages. The Hoe Library sale lasted through four years. The prize of the collection was a rare Gutenburg Bible, that had been knocked down to Bernard Quaritch, the London dealer, fourteen years previously for $20,000. It became the world's most expensive book (for many years) at $50,000, paid, as expected, by Huntington. When the total was announced—$1,932,000—it exceeded by a third the combined totals of the four most valuable libraries sold in England up to that time and was not beaten in America until the late 1960s.

It was not the end of Thomas E. Kirby's reign as the Million Dollar Voice, but it was the beginning of the decline. Although Arthur Swann quit Anderson's after the Hoe sale (he did not like some of Turner's business methods of persuasion) and joined the AAA, Kirby's control over his business was passing to his son, G. T. Kirby. It was

1. The black-pearl necklace and other jewellery from the Nina Dyer Collection which was sold by Christie's in Geneva for £1,236,264 ($9,592,639).

2. An American millionaire, Norton Simon,
bought Rembrandt's portrait of his son Titus.
for 760,000 guineas (nearly $2\frac{1}{4}$ m.) amid an
auction storm.

3. Augustus John—*Female Nude*, a typical
painting from the studio sale by Christie's.

4. Chagall—*The Shepherd* was sold for £15,185
in Tokyo on 27 May 1969 at the first sale ever
conducted by Western fine-art dealers in
Japan. The sale totalled more than £800,000.

5. Rouault—*The Lovers*, fetched £13,362 at the same sale in Tokyo. Both paintings were evidence of the surprising fascination found in Japan for Western Impressionists.

6. François Boucher, *La Fontaine d'Amour*. One of the pair traditionally held to have been painted by order of Madame de Pompadour for King Louis XV.

7. The other Boucher, *La Pipée aux Oiseaux*.
The pair, from the Dodge Collection and
both 116 × 133 in., sold for 400,000 guineas
($1,016,000).

8 and 9. ABOVE AND OPPOSITE: Velas-
quez's *Juan de Pareja*, sold at Christie's in 1970
for a record £2,310,000.

10. Then the most expensive piece of furniture ever sold. The Louis XVI bureau plat which belonged to the Grand Duchess Marie-Feodorovna, later the Czarina of Paul I. It came from the collection assembled by the late Mrs Anna Thomson Dodge, widow of the car manufacturer. It fetched 165,000 guineas ($415,800).

11. One of the pair of Louis XVI marquetry commodes made for a king's hunting lodge. Sold for 80,000 guineas ($200,000) from the Dodge collection. The clock is Louis XV.

12. BELOW: Titian was said to have put into *The Death of Actaeon* all the genius that God had given him. British art lovers, aided by the Government, put up £1,763,000 to save it for Britain after it had been sold to an American dealer at Christie's.

13 and 14. Claude Monet's painting, *La Terrasse à Sainte Adresse*, realized £588,000 ($1,411,000) in the 1960s Pitcairn sale. Van Dyck's *Four Negro Heads* fetched £420,000 at auction in 1972—ten times more than any Van Dyck painting had fetched before.

15. This Modigliani stone head, executed in
1910, reached a surprising £72,000 ($180,000)
at Sotheby's in the 1970s.

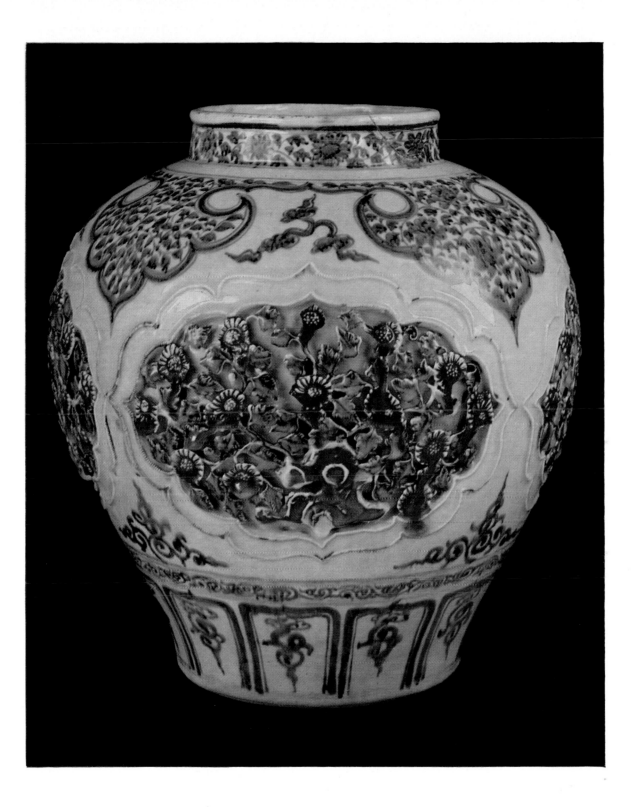

16. The rare, fourteenth-century Ming vase that was used as an umbrella stand and later sold for 210,000 guineas ($573,000).

17. Lady Blunt's Stradivarius violin, one of the three most beautiful in the world, sold at Sotheby's in 1971 for £84,000 ($201,600).

18. Twelfth-century bronze and silver-gilt statuette of St John, found by a farm worker in a field in Suffolk.

around this time that Otto Bernet and Major Hiram Parke came under the aegis of the AAA. Bernet had joined the galleries in 1896 at the traditional age of fourteen and in time became Kirby's stand-in auctioneer, although he never matched the silver tongue of the old barker nor the eloquence and class of Parke. The latter, who came from equally obscure origins (he was one of seven children of a dry-goods salesman) nevertheless grew into an imposing auctioneer. He acquired the rank of major in the National Guard and the title suited him. Somehow he let it stick. Kirby found him in Atlantic City, liked the look of his style and advanced him money for a divorce. He moved to New York and set up the Hiram Parke Galleries, financed by Kirby, to sell AAA rejects. He prospered. So too did the now implacable rivals, the Anderson Auction Company, now under the chairmanship of Mitchel Kennerley. Kennerley, originally a book publisher, inspired the Anderson to new heights, and made many a killing, particularly in the field of books. But he would sell anything, and would often stage seven different sales in a week. One of his coups was a $400,000 sale of Frederick R. Halsey's prints which took two and a half years.

In 1918 the Parke Gallery closed down and Parke joined the AAA as chief appraiser and occasionally, when Kirby would let him, auctioneer. Kirby was 'growing gray in honesty' as *Art News* wrote on his seventieth birthday, in a rather fulsome tribute, but he was also a cantankerous and obstinate old man who made life hell for both Parke and Bernet. Eventually his son, G. T. Kirby, persuaded him to move the AAA to new, fashionable quarters on Madison Avenue. G. T. spent $2,250,000 on building and equipment and in 1922 the move was made.

Kirby was seventy-six, and tired. Within six months he was deposed, the business sold to Cortlandt Field Bishop, a millionaire afficionado of the salerooms, and Parke and Bernet began a new era of drudgery in subordination to a new and even more demanding master. Bishop inherited millions from both sides of the family and spent all his life in a frenetic and largely successful attempt to spend them. He bought the AAA on a whim, and his whims spread far beyond the auction rooms. He bought the *Paris Times* because he didn't like the *Paris Herald*. He bought the Paris Ritz because the management once told him the suites were all filled. He bought a million dollars' worth of rare books and spent millions more on his travels to every quarter of the globe. He flooded Parke and Bernet with orders and instructions from all over the world and he despatched improbable cargoes to them to sell. But in spite of his imperious waywardness the AAA continued to prosper.

In 1927 Parke sold the Stillman collection for over $700,000, including Rembrandt's famous *Portrait of Titus* for $270,000. It held the world's auction record for a single painting for thirty-four years until

Rembrandt's *Aristotle Contemplating the Bust of Homer* fetched $2,300,000 at Parke–Bernet. The sale established Parke as America's first Gentleman of the Rostrum, erasing the memory of Kirby. It also relegated Bernet to the permanent position of Number Two, although the two vice-presidents of the Bishop empire had some way to go before they could claim it as their own. There is one picture of the two of them at Bishop's home, Lenox, in bowler hats. Parke is tall, white-moustachioed and suave; Bernet tubby, amiable and friendly. Between them is an Alsatian and the caption says viciously, 'Mr Bishop's Three Dogs.'

But for all their surface glitter, neither the AAA nor the Anderson

13. Major Hiram Parke conducts an auction at Parke–Bernet Galleries. He was the most dignified of auctioneers.

Galleries was doing well enough. The competition between them meant that each side was cutting commissions to the bone, leaving very little for profit. Bishop, estranged from his daughter, entered the first of a series of bitter lawsuits that was to dog him until he died, and Kennerley, who lived life to the full and past it, was in serious financial trouble himself. In 1927, after a series of convoluted negotiations in which Bishop cold-shouldered Parke and Bernet into the wings, he bought the Anderson galleries for $417,500, twice as much as Parke and Bernet estimated it was worth.

From then onwards Bishop played the two houses against one another, although ostensibly 'under the same management'. Each side had its successes. Parke sold the art treasures of Judge Elbert H. Gary, the banker who formed the American Steel Corporation with J. Pierpont Morgan, for an incredible $2,293,000, including $360,000 for Gainsborough's *The Harvest Waggon* and $245,000 for a little marble Houdon bust modelled after his infant daughter Sabine in 1788. Duveen had previously paid $100,000 for it in a Paris auction and sold it to Gary. He was expected to buy it, but faltered at the last. For Andersons, the sale of Jerome Kern's books in 1929 made $1,729,000. But in 1929, too, the stock market crashed.

Kennerley retired from the auction scene earlier that year and Bishop closed the Anderson Galleries and merged the two companies. With his usual penchant for doing the wrong thing he placed them both under the presidency of Milton Mitchell, Kennerley's former secretary and treasurer, and once more Parke and Bernet had to play second fiddle. Mitchell embarked on a series of disastrous flirtations with Spanish property sales and, as the depression deepened, took to drink. By 1933 he was sacked, leaving behind him a company with nearly $200,000 worth of debts and, at last, Bishop made Parke president and Bernet vice-president and went off on his travels again.

In 1935 Bishop died, leaving his affairs in the hands of his widow Amy and her constant companion over the years, Edith Nixon. The Bishop regime was replaced by a petticoat one no more acceptable to Parke and Bernet and, although the company's fortunes picked up under the expertise of the two old hands, Miss Nixon particularly disliked and did not trust Bernet. In 1937 the ladies proposed to reinstate Mitchell Kennerley as president of the AAA–AAC. Parke and Bernet quit at a stormy board meeting and as Parke told them he would, took their business with them. They had no capital, no premises, but a lifetime of auction experience behind them and the liking and trust of the hundreds of dealers and collectors they had worked with over the years.

Kennerley took over the old AAA–AAC and by 1938 it was sold to Milton Logan, formerly Bishop's private secretary, and an insurance broker, John T. Geery, for a down payment of $10,000 on a cash price of $185,000. The partnership led to nothing but grief. Logan was nearly killed in a murder attempt, Geery committed suicide and Logan was convicted for grand larceny. Kennerley lived on until he too committed suicide in 1950.

Parke–Bernet however, did prosper, even through the war years. By 1945, without any really spectacular sales, they had a virtual monopoly of the fine art and rare book market in the United States. Thanks largely to Bernet, who had the 'common touch', they compensated for the demise of the fabulous collectors of the 'tens and 'twenties by broadening their appeal to the public at large, proclaiming that for all the glamorous prices, 'hundreds of articles of relative rarity and genuine aesthetic merit were had for prices ranging from $25 to $100', thus pre-dating the British auction houses' claims of the 'sixties. O. B. Bernet died in 1945, his monument a seven-million-dollar turnover for the firm he had loved and served so well.

14. The present-day exterior of Parke–Bernet Galleries, New York.

By this time, the trio who were to guide Parke–Bernet's fortunes through the heady days of the booming 'fifties were firmly ensconced as Major Parke's aides-in-chief. Mary Vandegrift, the Pooh-Bah of the firm, did everything that no one else had time for, converting the Major's plans into action, running the publicity and co-ordinating the various departments. Louis Marion gradually took over as the replacement auctioneer; and Leslie Hyam catalogued and planned the great sales. They had all joined the firm before the war, and remained faithful to the Major when he split with Mrs Bishop. They all loved 'O. B.' as Bernet was fondly called, and they were all heart-broken when he departed from the galleries and when he died.

The 1948–9 season was Hiram Parke's last full one at the galleries. He conducted (with Marion) the big sale of the year, of the Joseph Brummer collection of early Christian and Byzantine antiquities which realized $739,000. In 1950 he left the responsibility for management in Hyam's hands and although he kept the chairmanship of the board of directors, he devoted himself more and more to his home and caring for his wife. He died in 1959, a month before the $2,000,000 Foy sale.

Parke–Bernet moved simultaneously into the 'fifties and into their current premises at 980 Madison Avenue. They also moved into a staggering new area of riches in the art market, matching and even surpassing the amazing scenes that were taking place in London as the world threw off the shackles of the war.

The climax came in the year 1957. In January Mrs Sarah Mae Cadwell Manwaring Plant Hayward Rovensky's possessions, the quan-tity of which nearly rivalled her names, were sold for $2,438,980 includ-ing a 213-carat diamond necklace which soared to $385,000. In the November, the collection of the opulent patrician financier from France, Georges Lurcy, who became an American millionaire many times over, fetched $2,221,000. Lurcy had died in 1953, but it was not until 1957 that his possessions came under the hammer by a Court Order. It was the first time that closed-circuit television had been used for a sale in America. Louis Marion, like everyone else, was confused by the echoing electronic bids, but 1,700 attended and the prices were outstanding. Renoir's *La Serre*, Lurcy's favourite paint-ing, for which he paid $24,000 in 1940, went to Henry Ford II for $200,000. Mr and Mrs Ford watched it all.

However, even Lurcy's sale was topped by Sotheby's in London with the Goldschmidt collection of Impressionists, when only seven paintings went for $2,186,800. And it was a sign of the times. For all their pride in their American origins and history, Parke–Bernet were under siege from across the Atlantic.

Meantime, they soared from success to success. In 1959 they sold the Foy collection of paintings and objets d'art, collected by the motor heiress, Thelma Chrysler Foy. It included seven Renoirs, one of which the French maestro of the art world, Durand-Ruel, had brought to Kirby's first exhibition at the old AAA in 1886. No one had wanted it then, and *Les Filles de Durand-Ruel* went back to France along with dozens of other masterpieces and sold to a man named Aude who married one of the two girls portrayed so lovingly by Renoir. In the mid-1940s the family sold it to a dealer for $15,000 and he passed it on to Mrs Foy.

Charles Durand-Ruel, great-nephew of the venerable dealer who had kept Renoir from starving, was there to bid for his aunts up to $224,000. Marion, the auctioneer, told his audience: 'I hate to see a good picture like that go so cheaply.' It eventually went to Walter P. Chrysler Jr., the late Mrs Foy's brother, for $255,000. The sale totalled $2,625,880.

The Erickson sale in 1961, including *Aristotle*, was Parke–Bernet's climacteric. $4,677,250 changed hands in one hour flat. Alfred W. Erickson, co-founder of the McCann–Erickson advertising agency, bought *Aristotle* from Duveen in the 'twenties for $750,000. After the 1929 crash he sold it back to Duveen for $500,000 and then, after business revived, bought it back a second time for $590,000. That year he died, and the picture, with its companions by Rembrandt, Van Dyck, Hals, Holbein and the rest finally came under the hammer

15. The sitter in Rembrandt's *Portrait of an Old Man* wearing a cap with a gold chain and an ostrich plume has undergone a variety of identifications since its first securely recorded appearance at a sale in Palmeira Square, Hove, in May 1877. When its new owner, a Hove collector called William Chamberlain, exhibited it at the Royal Academy in 1884 it had become 'Portrait of a Man-at-Arms'. At the time of his sale at Christie's in 1927 it was described as a 'Portrait of Rembrandt's Father, Harmen Gerrits van Rijn'. It is possible that it may have been sold at Christie's in 1811 as a 'Portrait of a Spanish General'. Today no one claims to know who the sitter is. He obviously interested the young Rembrandt very much, as the strong wiry features and firm, almost defiant expression appear several times in the early works. The enormous growth of interest in Rembrandt over the last 100 years is reflected in the vastly increasing sums the portrait has commanded on each successive occasion. Mr Chamberlain paid £100 for it in 1877. In 1927 Sir Edward Mountain bought it at Christie's for £7,000, a sum which brought spontaneous applause. When his son, Sir Brian Mountain, sold it on 5 December 1969 it was bought by Mr Edward Speelman for £315,000.

16. A 1970 sale of contemporary paintings at the Parke–Bernet Galleries, New York. John Marion is the auctioneer.

when his widow followed him in 1961. Fragonard's luscious *La Liseuse* went to the National Gallery in Washington for $875,000, Crivelli's *Madonna and Child* fetched $220,000, and fourth place went to Rembrandt's *Portrait of an Old Man* at $180,000.

It was nearly the end of yet another era. Sotheby's had competed strongly for the Erickson collection, as they had (successfully) for the Goldschmidt sale. Way back in 1949 they had made their initial approaches for control of Parke–Bernet and in the mid-fifties had set up their own offices in New York after Britain had eased currency restrictions. Throughout the early part of the 'sixties the battle waged on and a serious (and good) offer was turned down in 1962. But Peter Wilson, head of Sotheby's, persisted, and in 1964 he won.

In July of that year, the board finally accepted Peter Wilson's second offer, and this time the deal stuck. Since then, the combined firms have gone on from strength to strength, their combined yearly business totalling well over $100,000,000.

17. The most expensive car then sold. This 57SC Bugatti was sold at Sotheby–Parke–Bernet, Los Angeles, for $59,000 on 12 June 1971. The buyer, collector Dr Peter Williamson, a Connecticut neurosurgeon, commented: 'I never paid that much before for a Bugatti. I'm in a state of shock.' The underbidder (the one who lost) was Mr Rodney Clarke, a London collector who had originally sold the Bugatti to its last owner, Robert Oliver, in 1947 for $5,000.

18. The Diamond Necklace, 'property of a lady', which fetched £24,000 for the Red Cross at the start of the Second World War. It would be worth £250,000 in the 1970s.

The Second World War

The Second World War had much the same effect on the auction houses as had the First World War, in that staffs were reduced drastically by the demands of the armed forces and public attention was diverted to other, more urgent events than the sale of fine art. Sotheby's, however, had an easier time of it than Christie's, for the latter were heavily bombed in their King Street, London site in 1941 and were forced to spend the rest of the war in rented premises, struggling on as best they could with a skeleton staff. Sotheby's offered shelter to Christie's for the duration, but the offer was turned down, largely because it was felt that such a move could only lead to a loss of identity.

Mr Arthur Grimwade, one of Christie's directors, remembers the time well. He spent the first year or two of the war waiting for his call-up into the Navy, and performed many of the tasks that his seniors might have been required to undertake had they been available. For example, in order to catalogue its contents, he went to Woburn Abbey, the seat of the Duke of Bedford, before it was taken over by one of the Ministries ('Which one, we were never allowed to know . . .').

'This was in 1940,' he says. 'When we arrived at the foot of the steps to do the job, there were three pairs of footmen, each two steps higher than the last. The first would take our gloves and cases, the next our hats, and the last our coats. I remember that while we stayed there the newspapers came up to our rooms each morning *ironed*; and although there was no central heating, no matter at what time of the day or night we went to our rooms there would be a log fire blazing and a jug of boiling hot water waiting for us to use for washing . . .'

In that first year Christie's went back to their old job of the First World War—running Red Cross sales. At first, there was a great series of sales which totalled around £70,000 for a whole mass of varying items sent in by the public.

The American Ambassador to London at the time was Mr Joseph Kennedy, father of the former President of the United States. He went to a preview of the silver sale and took a strong fancy to a silver-gilt tea service that had been contributed to the Red Cross by Queen Elizabeth (now the Queen Mother). It had been designed for the twenty-fifth anniversary of the reign of her father-in-law, King George V.

Mr Kennedy went to the sale and bought the tea service. 'Now I can invite the Queen to tea,' he said, 'and she can have tea from her own tea service.'

Another famous lady, who is anonymous even now, over thirty years later, donated a superb diamond necklace, which was sold for £24,000. At values in the 1970s, it would easily fetch a quarter of a million pounds.

One night in 1941 a number of incendiary bombs fell on Christie's in King Street and burnt the old building to the ground. The famous salerooms were destroyed, but most of the valuables and the records were in an underground strongroom beneath the building and were unharmed, apart from some water damage. Christie's moved to Derby House, the empty town house of the Earls of Derby, and remained in business there and in Stanley House, another famous London residence, until after the war. But it was not until 1953 that the premises were rebuilt and King Street became the dignified salerooms we know today.

19. Arthur Grimwade's own photograph of the ruin left by German bombers of Christie's premises in King Street in April 1941.

20. Clearing the site.
21. Christie's being rebuilt after the Second
World War.

22. An illustration from J. J. Audubon's
Birds of America.

The 'Forties
Sotheby's Audubon

In 1922, the estate of the nineteenth-century heiress, Baroness Burdett-Coutts, sold at Sotheby's a collection of 448 Audubon engravings of 'Birds of America' for £200. In 1969, forty-seven years later, the same set was presented again for sale—and this time it fetched £90,000, a world record price.

Audubon's bird book has always been considered an extraordinary accomplishment. The self-taught artist–ornithologist achieved what no predecessor—or successor—was able to do. He painted the known species of birds in the United States and Canada from life, in their natural habitat. Furthermore, he had them magnificently engraved—life-size—and exquisitely hand-coloured. Perhaps his greatest achievement was that he managed to complete his undertaking. He delivered the eighty-seventh and final five-plate part, finishing the set of 435 plates, in 1838, eleven years after the first part was published.

The set sold at Sotheby's is almost certain to be one which Audubon made for his wife Lucy's well-to-do cousin, Miss Euphemia Gifford, of Duffield Bank, Derby. When she first ordered her set in April 1831 Audubon had written to her assuring her of his gratitude for her patronage. He and his wife had earlier named their first child Victor Gifford Audubon, after Miss Gifford. After she died in about 1853 it is believed the set passed from her estate to Miss Burdett-Coutts, then thirty-nine and the richest heiress in Britain. The extra thirteen plates were pulled after the complete work of 435 plates was finished, in order to correct slight errors in attribution that had crept into Audubon's mammoth work. And finally, specially for Miss Gifford, Audubon designed and had made a unique mahogany chest of drawers, one for each of the four volumes, to hold the set, preserving it in pristine condition.

Thanks to an anonymous donor, the set is now in Field Museum of Natural History, Chicago.

23. Cézanne: *Garçon au Gilet Rouge*
(£220,000).

The 'Fifties
The Sale of the Century

The years after the Second World War were comparatively thin ones so far as the great sales houses were concerned. Food and fuel rationing, rehabilitation and re-establishment affected Britain as well as most of Europe; and with currency restrictions and grey-faced purpose setting the *modus vivendi* of the times, the Iron Curtain and the Cold War over-shadowed such pastimes as buying, selling and collecting.

By 1954, however, the world was returning to something like normal, and the long-established expertise of the London sales personnel began to flex its muscles for the astonishing boom which was triggered off by the removal of restrictions on the import of works of art from the United States. At the same time, it became possible once again to pay the seller *in his own currency*, and the Americans responded.

Sotheby's were the first to capitalize on the new freedoms. In 1956 they staged their first sale of French Impressionist pictures which had been collected by the late Jacob Goldschmidt of New York, and fifty-six paintings were sold in ninety-three minutes for a total of $912,800. But the climax came in the 1958–9 season, when prices soared, record after record was broken, and Sotheby's staged what must be the definitive 'Sale of the Century' on the night of 15 October 1958, when the second batch from the Goldschmidt collection was sold.

This was the sale which re-established London as the leading art centre of the world. From then on paintings, jewellery and objets d'art have flowed into London from all over the world. Here, say international dealers, you not only get the best prices, but you're likely to get the best deal too.

That night was one to remember. There were only seven paintings on offer, and they made the (then) shattering figure of £781,000. It was the first time Sotheby's had staged a major sale in the evening, and an atmosphere of tension, rather like that of a first-night, hung over the salerooms. Over 1,200 people crammed into the salerooms, admission was by ticket only, and closed-circuit television took the sale into every nook and cranny of Sotheby's—even to the basement.

The first bid was taken at nine o'clock, and twenty minutes later it was all over.

Cézanne's *Garçon au Gilet Rouge* had made £220,000, the highest price ever paid for a picture at auction at that time, and one which many 'experts thought would never be beaten.' The same artist's *Les*

Grosses Pommes made £90,000 even though a London barrow-boy had been quoted in the Press as saying 'I wouldn't sell them apples for eighteen pence a pound.' Manet's *La Rue du Berne, Manet à la Palette* and *La Promenade* fetched £113,000, £89,000 and £65,000. They had been sold in the nineteenth century for £20, £60, and £40 respectively. Van Gogh's *Jardin Public à Arles*, which is thought to be one of four pictures painted as a decoration for Gauguin's visit to Arles in October 1889, made £132,000 a record for a Van Gogh until 25 February 1970, when Sotheby–Parke–Bernet sold Van Gogh's *Les Cyprès et l'arbres en fleurs* for £541,666. The only picture out of the seven to remain in Britain was Renoir's *La Pensée*, of which the artist had rather unkindly remarked, 'Why has this title been given to my picture—that girl never thought, she lived like a bird and nothing more.' It made £72,000.

Books were next in the news, on 1 December 1958. This was the

24.   Cézanne: *Les Grosses Pommes* (£90,000).

incredible sale of forty-five illuminated manuscripts, a block book and three printed books from the Dyson Perrins Collection—fifty lots—which averaged £6,500 each and totalled £326,620, the biggest single book sale in the world. Previously the world's most expensive book had been the *Bedford Book of Hours*, bought by the American magnate J. Pierpont Morgan in 1929 for £33,000 and sold at cost price to the British Museum, where it remains to this day.

The Dyson Perrins sale beat this three times. Mr H. P. Kraus, a well-known American book dealer, paid £39,000 for a mid-twelfth-century book of Latin Gospels, £36,000 was paid for a French thirteenth-century Bestiary, and the Swiss National Museum paid £33,000 for the Gradual of the Dominican Nuns of St Catherenthal, Switzerland (early fourteenth-century).

As if these two events were not enough for one season, the climax came when, in order to raise death duties, the executors of the late

25. Manet: *La Rue de Berne* (£113,000).

26.   Manet: *Manet à la Palette* (£89,000).

27.   Manet: *La Promenade* (£65,000).

28.   Renoir: *La Pensée* (£72,000).

29.   Mr Leonard Koetzer, a London dealer,
bought the *Adoration of the Magi* by Rubens
at Sotheby's for £275,000. It is now at King's
College, Cambridge.

30.   The Duchess of Westminster's Tiara—it
fetched £110,000, a British record.

Duke of Westminster's vast estates decided to send certain pictures, furniture, silver, jewellery and other works of art to Sotheby's for sale. They included one of Rubens' finest works, *The Adoration of the Magi*—until then the most important single picture to be auctioned.

It was painted in Antwerp in 1634 for the Convent of the Dames Blanches and Rubens was paid 920 florins for it (roughly £74). When the convents were suppressed in 1783 the picture was sold (by auction!) in Brussels on 18 September 1785 and was purchased by one Jean Baptiste Horion for 8,400 florins. In 1788 Horion sold it again—to 'Donckers, pour Angleterre', and it appeared later in a sale of the Marquess of Landsdowne's property and was bought by the then Lord Grosvenor for £800. The artist is said to have painted it in only eleven days. It is the only altar-piece by Rubens in England.

Before coming to Sotheby's it had been hanging in Eaton Hall, one of the late Duke of Westminster's homes, where it had fortunately survived the attentions of members of the Officer Training Corps who had been stationed there during the Second World War.

The picture was too large to be brought to the salerooms in the usual way. It measured 12 ft by 8 ft. So a hole had to be cut in the floor of one of the galleries and the picture was lifted through it several weeks before the sale was due to take place, and thousands of people went to see it. There was of course a great deal of speculation as to who would buy it, and the general consensus was that it would be an American museum or art gallery. Questions were asked in Parliament whether or not an export licence would be granted, but the result surprised everyone. The *Adoration* was bought for £275,000, up to then a world record for any painting, by a London art dealer, Mr Leonard Koetzer, who blandly announced that he had bought it on behalf of an English private collector and it would remain in Britain. It now hangs in the chapel of King's College, Cambridge.

The sale itself totalled £740,000, then a world record for Old Master paintings. It included a portrait of the *Apostle St James the Great* by El Greco, which made £72,000, and a self-portrait of the painter Frans Hals which fetched £48,000. There was also a little panel of the Resurrection by Rubens, that had been sent in by a convent. It had been offered to a dealer for £100, for the convent was short of funds, but he, good fellow, thought it was worth more and advised the Reverend Mother to send it to Sotheby's. It fetched £31,000.

Next day Sotheby's sold the Westminster Tiara for £110,000, the highest price paid for a piece of jewellery in Britain. The two centre stones, known as the Arcot diamonds, had once been presented to Queen Charlotte by the Nawab Azim-ud-daula. In her will the Queen directed that the jewels should be sold, and they were bought by the Marquess of Westminster for his wife; total cost, £14,000.

31. Painted on a door in Tahiti—Gauguin's
Standing Girl.

The 'Sixties
Sotheby's

For years, Frank Davis, doyen of London Art Correspondents, wrote the review of the year in Sotheby's *Art at Auction*, that annual and expensive record of the sales of the year. The details of the provenance, the beauty and the cost of each item fascinated him; but so too did the 'ambience' which, snobbish though it may be, has not failed to captivate shrewd and cynical journalists just as much in the twentieth century as it did in the eighteenth.

Take this snatch from 1961:

'It is long since auctioneers in London attempted eloquence either vocally or in print. Sound scholarship in the compilation of a catalogue is worth all the glib sales talk in the world; this was an article of faith laid down a century ago when Sotheby's sold only books, and has been one of the pillars upon which the reputation of the firm has been built. Short-sighted art dealers—not of course the good ones—have more than once complained to me "Sotheby's, oh! yes, we have to go there, but they over-catalogue"—by which they mean that nearly all the information is given and not just a part of it. Specialist speculators like to read vague descriptions, with as little past history as possible. I have even met a dealer who spoke sourly of the engaging Black Museum behind the scenes of the Ceramics Department—a little collection gathered together over the years for the edification of young and old so that as few clever forgeries should slip through the net as possible. However, an unknown paid this little collection a handsome compliment; he stole a piece from it, convinced presumably that it was genuine.

'The more innocent visitors tell me that they find the place at first glance startlingly casual—it is not just the unemphatic voice from the rostrum, but the apparent higgledy-piggledy display, the sprawling, dead-pan audience creeping in and out, the paintings hung from floor to ceiling, the dust of ages, almost the odour of sanctity; everything played down, they say, as if each actor in the drama were determined to throw away his lines. All this, no doubt, is true enough, though unrehearsed; just an old Spanish custom, as it were, which, combined with an underlying efficiency of which this record is sufficient witness, has grown up with the years. This efficiency, by common sense out of expertise, has long been recognized abroad and accounts for the

32. *Le Loing à Moret, et Eté* by Alfred Sisley.
32,000 guineas ($94,080). This work was
among forty-five Impressionist and post-
Impressionist paintings belonging to Mr and
Mrs John Boulton of Caracas, Venezuela,
sold by Christie's in December of 1965. The
collection was formed by Mr Boulton's father,
who, although living in Caracas, made fre-
quent visits to Paris between 1922 and 1930,
often accompanied by the painter Manuel
Cabre. The collection had remained un-
altered since its formation and in the case
of thirty-two of the pictures the original bills
of sale had been preserved. These thirty-two,
which included works by Bonnard, Chagall,
Dufy, Kisling, Laurencin, Monet, Pissarro,
Soutine, Utrillo and others cost Mr Boulton
Senior £3,789. At the auction they achieved
a total of £136,143 ($383,200) a 3,500 per
cent increase. The collection altogether made
£216,153 ($605,229).

high proportion of goods of every sort which their owners consider
worth despatch from Europe and from across the Atlantic for sale—
sales which account for about thirty per cent of the total turnover.'

That season two sales dominated the scene. The first, in April,
saw thirty-five pictures from the collection of Somerset Maugham,
the author, sold for more than £500,000 at Sotheby's. They included

a superb piece of board which happened to be decorated on both sides by Picasso (over £100,000), two Renoirs at £48,000 each and £28,000 for a Pissarro (the first time this remarkable artist had been recognized so highly). Frank Davis wrote:

'No one can pretend that the door which Gauguin painted in Tahiti—*The Standing Girl*—and which Maugham acquired in 1916 when he was visiting the Island for 200 Francs (the picture, not the visit)—was the master's greatest achievement; but it made £13,000, admittedly a great deal less than the royalties which flowed in over the years from the novel and film from *The Moon and Sixpence*, the literary result of that visit.'

Sisley's riverscape at Moret painted in 1880 was sold for £30,000—in 1880 Sisley was pledging landscapes with the local baker in order to keep his family alive; and the unusual and magnificent nude by Toulouse-Lautrec, *Le Polisseur*, was secured by America for £27,000.

The second evening sale was that of the collection of Sir Alexander Korda, the film giant, at which Monet's *La Barque Bleue* made £56,000. One Degas nude made £72,000, and a pastel of two women in conversation fetched £24,000. The total: just under the half-million pounds.

These prices were, however, quickly exceeded the following year, when the William Cargill collection of forty-eight Impressionist paintings made more than £1,000,000 at Sotheby's.

William Cargill was a crotchety, reticent Scot who was a member of the very rich Cargill family that made most of its money in Far Eastern enterprises; he proved to be a shrewd buyer of Impressionist paintings in the early 'twenties when innovators like Monet and Renoir were not at all fashionable. Other members of the family gave generously to the City of Glasgow and to Glasgow University, but William seemed determined to carry on a war with Glasgow Corporation, one which appears to have been returned with interest, and so after his death his marvellous collection was dispersed all over the world from Sotheby's Rooms in London.

Dr T. J. Honeyman, then Director of the Glasgow Art Gallery and Museum, wrote in *Scottish Field* in July 1963 that most of the paintings that Cargill acquired during the 'thirties were still in their packing-cases—concealed in wardrobes or under the beds in various out-of-use bedrooms.

He wrote:

'I was allowed to sort out the collection, tidy things up generally and hang the paintings in some kind of order . . . for all of us on the Arts side at Kelvingrove it was an exciting experience. . . Of course, I was hoping that eventually he would emulate my friend, William McInnes, whose magnificent bequest had helped to raise the

33. *La Ruisseau à Osny* by Camille Pissarro, signed and dated '83. From the collection of Mr and Mrs John Boulton of Venezuela. Bought in 1922 for £560; sold in December 1965 for 26,000 guineas ($76,400).

34.   Picasso—*Maternité au Bord de la Mer.*

importance of the civic art collection to international level. Two things killed that hope. The first was the Corporation's decision to elevate the Museum side at the expense of the Art side. Cargill's comment was: "They don't seem to think much of their art collection." Long afterwards Cargill was persuaded to lend six of his paintings to the Glasgow Fine Art Institute. He agreed on condition his name must not appear and that the paintings must be hung in a group. The committee thought that the Gauguin of the *Three Breton Girls* (Cargill paid £3,200 for it; it sold for £75,000) was not very typical and they couldn't find room for two others. The Corporation is not alone in the possession of blind spots. . .'

Whatever the worthy doctor thought about the Corporation, there is no doubt that the art world confirmed his opinion of the paintings. In 1928 Cargill had paid £4,200 for Degas' *Danseuse Basculante*; now it made £105,000. In 1939 he paid £12,800 for the same master's *La Repetition sur la Scene*— now £55,000. Pissarro's *Charing Cross Bridge* of 1890 cost him £2,600 in 1937 (£47,000) and in the same year he bought Sisley's *Entrée de Village* for £1,500 plus £20 for the frame. In 1963 it fetched £24,500.

By 1967 the prices paid for Impressionists had begun to soar beyond belief. In April of that year one of Sotheby's sales brought in over £1,000,000. The major work was a Picasso, the tender, compassionate *Maternité au Bord de la Mer* which Picasso painted in Barcelona in 1902. It was originally given to a Dr Fontbona in payment for medical services and is inscribed to him. Now it was sold for £190,000—by far the highest sum given anywhere for a work by a living painter. Had it not been for that formidable figure, more fuss might have been made about the £145,000 paid for a Cézanne still life—and only four of the eighty-six paintings on sale went for less than £1,000.

In July of the same year, Sotheby's held something of a family occasion—Sir Chester Beatty sent over ten of his paintings from Dublin. He had played an important part in encouraging the then senior Sotheby partner, Sir Montague Barlow, to move to New Bond Street and inject new life into the old book business. The ten paintings fetched £242,000—presumably justifying Sir Chester's faith.

The 'Sixties
The Berkeley Castle Silver

The Berkeley Castle silver dinner service of 168 pieces was sold at Sotheby's on 16 June 1960. It was made by the famous Jacques Roettier in 1734 for the Earl of Berkeley, and had never left the Castle since that date.

Sotheby's silver experts had been to the castle to value the remaining silver for sale, but when they asked about the dinner service were told: 'Oh, you won't get anything for that, we use it every day!' In fact, it was insured for £3,000; but even before the sale a bid of £50,000 was made for it. Sotheby's advice was for it to be sold as one lot at auction. The sale lasted two minutes twenty seconds and the service was knocked down to a London dealer, Frank Partridge, against spirited French bidding. The price: £207,000 ($520,000).

35. The Berkeley Castle silver service—'We use it every day, it can't be worth much.' Not even £207,000?

36. *The Judgement of Paris* by Rubens.
Offered on sale in November 1966, it failed
to reach its reserve price. It was subsequently
acquired by the National Gallery, London,
for an undisclosed price.

The 'Sixties
The Rubens Poker Game

Robert Savage started business in 1905 as a picture framer with his wife Eva on £5 capital and a great deal of hope. He never made much money, and when he died in 1951 his widow lived on in very modest circumstances in a terrace house in Northampton until one day in 1966 she was visited by a representative of Christie's.

It had been part of Robert Savage's business to buy up old frames which he would regild. In 1933 he bought a wagon-load of frames from a dealer in York named Calter, at an average price of ten shillings each. Calter threw in the pictures to clinch the deal.

The Savages could never bear to throw paintings away. 'They cluttered up the workshop, and I had to forbid my husband to keep any more', Mrs Savage recalled. The result was a considerable collection of about 1,000 pictures, and eventually, in 1966, Mrs Savage sent forty of them to Christie's for sale. One of them, from the York job lot, was a Rubens, the long-lost *Judgment of Paris*.

'Robert, my late husband, always knew that picture had quality,' said Mrs Savage, unsurprised, when the experts told her of her unknown treasure.

In fact, Christie's nearly missed it—unusually for them. The picture went through the first stage of their attribution machinery, which deals with several hundred pictures each week, and was thought to be the work of a late seventeenth-century copyist called Lankrink. As such, it was hung for sale in a routine way. However, it had been spotted previously by Oliver Millar, the Deputy Surveyor of the Queen's Paintings, a specialist in early seventeenth-century paintings and one of the small élite of the art world whom Christie's and other major auctioneers encourage to browse through their storerooms (you never know what you've missed). Millar saw the picture in the store, and it stirred his interest. When he went back to have a second look, it was already hanging on the wall of the 'Great Room' as 'Lot 183: Lankrink: *The Judgment of Paris*.' This time he had no doubt (in the good light) and went to find David Carritt, the firm's Old Master director, who had not up to that moment seen it. 'Isn't that a rather important picture you've got in your sale?' he asked. Carritt dashed into the Great Room. 'My God!' he said after one look.

A snap meeting of directors decided to leave the picture hanging;

it would in any case be interesting to see how the art world reacted. Meanwhile Mrs Savage was advised the picture should be withdrawn from the sale for further attribution.

The delicate poker-game then followed which was a classic of its kind. Some top dealers sensed there was something in the air, but everyone was playing it cool in the hope of snapping up a bargain. Unusual numbers of dealers thronged through Christie's daily, studiously avoiding looking directly at *The Judgment*. Sir Philip Hendy, then Director of the National Gallery, went twice to have a look, made discreet telephone calls and stole in to examine it closely from behind a conveniently placed screen. There wasn't much left of the Gallery's budget for the year, but to get a Rubens for a song would be a magnificent coup.

Christie's watched all this with some amusement, but the dealers were not so happy when, at the picture sale next day, the 'Lankrink' was withdrawn.

The delay gave the experts time to complete their detective work. They became convinced that it was an important early work by Rubens, painted around 1600, the year when Rubens was made court painter to the Duke of Mantua. There is a pen drawing in the Louvre, dated 1600, which appears to be a preliminary sketch for the large figure of Paris, offering the golden apple to the Three Graces. Such a picture could well have been projected for the Duke of Mantua, but there is some evidence that Rubens kept it. A note by his executors refers to a painting of the *Three Graces* (an alternative title for *The Judgment of Paris*) about 6 ft by 4 ft. The description does not seem to apply to any previously known painting by Rubens and this one is 5 ft 9 in by 4 ft 4 in. According to the executors, Rubens' first wife so disliked the picture that it was sold off—so they believe—to an agent of the King of England. That would have been Endymion Porter, who bought for Charles I. This gave a valid hypothesis for the picture reaching England. Although it does not bear the royal stamp CP which identifies pictures from Charles' collection, it is a fact that the King did not accept everything that Porter sent him. *The Three Graces* could have been given away—pictures frequently made royal wedding-presents.

Another clue dates from 1825, when John, fourth Earl of Darnley, commissioned William Etty to paint him a version of *The Judgment of Paris* for £500. The result, which now hangs in the Leverhulme Art Gallery, looks very much as though Etty drew very heavily from Rubens.

All this of course, meant little to Mrs Savage. At eighty-two, she knew there were more important things than mere money.

'I would like to settle something on the family,' she said. 'But most of all I would like it to be bought by someone who would let people see it. Then people would say "That's the picture Robert Savage had." He would have liked that.'

At the sale, bidding stopped at around £80,000—short of the reserve that was placed on it. But now the picture hangs in Britain's National Gallery in Trafalgar Square, and Mrs Savage's wish comes daily true.

Strangely enough, another early Rubens turned up at the same sale and fetched £24,000. It was an enchanting sketch for *Samson and Delilah* which is in the Neuberg collection at Hamburg. It is on a panel, and shows Samson having his locks shorn while he sleeps at Delilah's feet with his head on her lap. Armed Philistines can be seen in the half-opened doorway waiting to seize Samson.

It, too, was bought in the 1930s in York for a few pounds, and remained unrecognized by its owner until he took it into Christie's for sale.

The 'Sixties
Nina, the Green-eyed Goddess

Once upon a time, a beautiful English girl went off to the French Riviera to catch a millionaire. She caught two—a German Baron and a Moslem Prince. Both showered her with jewels but she found no happiness. She committed suicide, and her jewels were sold in what was then the biggest jewellery sale of the century.

It sounds like a fairy story, or the plot for a tragic opera. It is a true-life tale of our times, however. The English girl was Nina, whose background was as stormy as her life. Her father was a British electrical company executive, William Aldrich, who married her mother, Elsie, in England in 1923. One day in 1929 he came home from a business trip to find that Elsie had gone to the apartment of a retired tea planter, Stanley Dyer.

He begged Elsie to come back to him, which she did for a short while. Then she left him to join Dyer permanently and Nina was born the next February. He later told the British courts that Elsie pleaded with him not to sue for a divorce 'for the sake of our baby.'

In any case, Dyer took Elsie and Nina with him to Ceylon, where he died in 1945 and Elsie in 1954. When Nina was twelve, however, her mother had sent her back to England to study acting, at which she proved to be a poor student. She graduated into fashion modelling by day and more dubious employment in nightclubs at night; but at twenty she took off for France, telling the other girls at the fashion house: 'I'm off to catch me a millionaire.'

It took her four years. In 1954 she married Baron von Thyssen. His family possessed a German steel fortune second only to that of Krupps, but it couldn't hold Nina. The marriage lasted ten months. Two years later along came Prince Sadruddin Khan, whose father, then the Aga Khan, was weighed in gold and diamonds by his followers. He was a plump man. Nina said she wanted children, but instead she received more gems; and her second marriage lasted five years. She often said she thought of killing herself but she couldn't pluck up the courage. In 1965, she did.

Her husbands, both of them numbered among the ten richest men in the world, could not give her happiness, but they gave her love, marriage—and jewels (colour plate 1). Her three-strand black-pearl necklace to which both contributed is believed to be unique. One strand has forty-nine pearls weighing 787·44 grains; a second has the same number but slightly smaller at 644·72 grains and the third has fifty-three pearls totalling 979·52 grains.

With the necklace, Nina wore in each ear a vast black pearl set off with diamonds. When European jewellers first saw them, some wondered whether the pearls were genuine. But they have been submitted to every known test. And they are solid pearl, black all through.

Apart from pearls, love brought Nina two diamond rings, one of thirty-two carats and the other of twenty-nine, and emeralds by the score. Nina loved wild animals. Von Thyssen gave her a baby black leopard and then he had made for her leopard-shaped ornaments with diamonds and sapphires for spots to decorate her wrist, her gown, her fingers. There was a Siamese cat in black enamel set with diamonds.

Even in death, Nina couldn't get things right. The once obscure model, who had kept the gossip columns humming throughout the 1950s, came alone to her Paris house one night in 1965 and took an overdose of drugs. She left behind notes decreeing that her estate go to wild-life funds and animal homes in Africa and Europe. But by now she had become a Swiss citizen, and Swiss law decrees that if there are living relatives, the estate cannot go to charity. So Nina's father, William Aldrich, fought a four-year battle in the courts to establish his claim. And won.

And so on 1 May 1969, Christie's held a sale in Geneva. It was an occasion glittering with social prestige as much as commercial value. The front row of seats, facing Mr Ivan Chance who conducted the auction himself in French, was filled by some of the richest people in the world. Among them were Ortiz Patino of the Brazilian tin family, the Maharajah the Gaekwar of Baroda, the Princess of Liechtenstein and the Archdukes Josef and Michael of Austria.

The hotel ballroom holds under 400. That 1 May, 800 crowded in and an overflow audience watched proceedings and made their bids by closed-circuit television. Within minutes the temperature, under the television lights, reached ninety-five degrees. Emotionally, it was charged to boiling-point. Top price of the sale went to a single-stone mounted diamond ring which fetched £120,000 ($276,000). Harry Winston of New York, world famous diamond merchant had made it for Nina. That night he bought it back. The fabulous pearls, however, didn't sell and were bought in for £70,000 ($133,000)—about one third of the estimated figure.

Christie's, who's security operation was so large that they issued a statement denying that the Swiss Army was on manoeuvre in the area specially for the occasion, paid tribute to Nina's memory. They charged seven dollars a head for the preview and gave the proceeds to the World Wild-Life Fund, so dear to Nina's heart.

But Sadruddin Khan, who once gave the little green-eyed girl from Ceylon an island as a wedding present, wasn't there. Nor was the German steel Baron.

37. Van Gogh—*Portrait de la Mère de l'Artiste.*

The 'Sixties
The Luck of Theodore Pitcairn

Theodore Pitcairn was born in Philadelphia just before the turn of the century, with two enormous advantages over the average person. In the first place, his father was one of the founders of the Pittsburgh Glass Company, one of the largest firms in the United States—two places behind Coca Cola, or thereabouts. Secondly, he liked Impressionist paintings at a time when these manifestations of artistic ability were, if not frowned upon, at least regarded with suspicion as not quite the right thing.

Young Theodore grew up to be a remarkable individual. He was ordained a minister of the mystical General Church of New Jerusalem (Swedenborgian) in Bryn Athyn, Pennsylvania in 1918, and then spent several years in charge of a mission station in Basutoland. He returned to the United States in 1926 to found the Lord's New Church at Bryn Athyn and serve there as a pastor until he retired in 1962. In 1926, too, he married, and has nine children and eleven grandchildren. Throughout the 1920s he indulged, if that is the right word, in his passion for collecting paintings. He started in 1921, when he paid twenty thousand dollars (around £7,000) for three works by Vincent Van Gogh—*Portrait of Mademoiselle Ravoux*, *Le Semeur* and a pencil drawing: *Sorrow*.

'At the time some people thought I was rather queer as he wasn't too well known,' said Mr Pitcairn in 1966, when the three works had been sold for a total of £246,000 ($660,000). What people thought has never worried the Rev. Theodore too much. In all, in 1965 and 1966 he sold six paintings at Christie's for just under a million pounds ($2,430,000). They were:

La Terrasse à Sainte Adresse by Claude Monet (colour plate 13), £588,000 ($1,411,000)
Portrait de la Mère de l'Artiste by Van Gogh, £115,500 ($277,000)
Sorrow (drawing) by Van Gogh, £11,500 ($32,400)
Portrait de Mlle Ravoux by Van Gogh, £157,000 ($441,000)
Le Semeur by Van Gogh, £78,750 ($189,000)
La Berge à Sainte-Mammes by Alfred Sisley, £42,000 ($100,800)

'I stopped buying paintings years ago because prices were going up and there were very few of the more recent ones that I care for,' he said after the sale of the Monet, which broke all existing records

38. *Sorrow* by Van Gogh. Sold from the collection of the Rev Theodore Pitcairn of Bryn Athyn, Pennsylvania for 11,000 guineas ($32,400).

39. *Portrait de Mademoiselle Ravoux* by Van Gogh. From the Pitcairn collection, this sold for a then record price for the artist, £157,500 ($441,000) at Christie's in 1966. Van Gogh described it in a letter to his brother Theo written on 24 June 1890, five weeks before his death. He wrote: 'Last week I did a portrait of a girl about sixteen in blue against a blue background, the daughter of the people with whom I am staying. I have given her this portrait, but I made a variant of it for you, a size 15 canvas.' (Mlle Ravoux was the daughter of the owner of the Café Ravoux, Place de la Marie, Auvers-sur-Oise where Van Gogh stayed from 21 May 1890 and where he died on 29 July.)

40. Van Gogh—*Le Semeur*.

for an Impressionist work. 'I have never bought a painting for any other reason than that I liked it.' Among his paintings Mr Pitcairn has works by a Dutch artist named Philippe Smit, but he concedes that there is practically no market in Smits and even if a boom were to develop, there is at least one Smit in his home that would never sell. 'I came to know Smit many years ago when I met him at his studio in Holland,' says Mr Pitcairn. 'I bought a pastel he had done of a young girl. I told him I'd like to see the girl who posed for it. I met her. She was nearly sixteen. Four or five years later I married her.'

La Terrasse marks a watershed in art history. Monet painted it in 1867 and it is universally accepted as the forerunner of Impressionism. He was in financial straits at the time and he was compelled to take refuge with his father and his aunt, both of whom had houses at the little village of Sainte Adresse, which has long since been absorbed into Le Havre. It was at one of these houses that Monet painted the picture. The man seated in the chair is believed to be Monet's father, the woman next to him his aunt, Mme Lecadre; the two standing figures Dr Lecadre and his daughter; and the whole picture, although almost academic by comparison with Monet's later work, is drenched in light.

A little later Monet, still very hard up, sold the painting to a Paris dealer, M. Prat, for 400 francs—then worth about £15 ($40). M. Prat's widow sold it for 40,000 francs to Durand-Ruel, and Monet was understood to have wanted to buy it back. By then, however, it was 1913, and the painting was at Durand-Ruel Gallery in New York, where it was eventually bought by Mr Pitcairn.

He described how he bought it. 'I remember it was a beautiful day and my wife and I were walking down 57th Street, New York, when we saw the painting. We bought it there and then because we liked it. The way its value has appreciated I consider extraordinary even though it is a wonderful painting.'

The Christie's sale price—£588,000 ($1,411,000)—represented a 30,000 per cent profit. It now hangs in the Metropolitan Museum, New York.

41. On the death of Augustus Edwin John, the contents of the artist's studio were auctioned by Christie's. A self-portrait (above) by this outstanding British portrait painter fetched £33,405, and other paintings made lesser sums. A typical female nude from the sale is shown in colour plate 3. The total reached in the two sales, held in 1962 and 1963, was £100,170.

The 'Sixties
Titus, the Boy who Moved Hearts

On 19 March 1965, the painting which has moved more hearts possibly than any other, Rembrandt's portrait of his son, *Titus* (colour plate 2) was sold to Mr Norton Simon of Los Angeles for 760,000 guineas ($2,234,000), at the time a world record for a single picture.

It had been for around 150 years in Britain, and the story of how it came there is told by the Spencer family. It seems that George Barker, a picture restorer and dealer, missed his boat home from Holland and was obliged to pass the night at a farmhouse outside the Hague. In the morning he discovered, hanging on his bedroom wall, a Rembrandt portrait of superlative beauty. When he expressed his admiration for it to his host, the amiable farmer offered to throw it in with the price of bed and breakfast—one shilling.

Barker was so pleased with his bargain that on the way to the harbour to catch his boat he got down from his carriage and sat in a public garden to examine the picture. He was sitting lost in its beauties when a man riding by drew close, looked over his shoulder and then dismounted.

'You have a picture of my ancestor there,' he said. 'That is Prince William of Orange as a boy.' The horseman was none other than the King of the Netherlands.

Back in England, Barker presented 'Prince William' to his patron, Lord Spencer, whose wife Lavinia found it so beautiful that she said: 'This picture must never leave the house.'

But in 1915 Sir Herbert Cook paid £60,000 for it and fifty years later it was put up for auction at Christie's by his son, Sir Francis.

Apart from the price, the sale itself caused something of a sensation. It certainly afforded Mr Ivan Chance, Christie's Chairman at the time, the 'most embarrassing moment of my life.' It happened like this.

Mr Simon, the eventual buyer, was there early, choosing a seat at the front of the crowded auction room on the right-hand side of the auctioneer's rostrum. Mr David Somerset, of Marlborough Fine Art and Sir Geoffrey Agnew, of Agnew's, both major London dealers, were there too, waiting.

Bidding started at 100,000 guineas. In four seconds it was up to 200,000, in six up to 300,000 and in ten seconds it reached 400,000. All three bidders were bidding vocally. No secret signs were used.

Mr Somerset reached his price of 740,000 guineas in a minute and a half, eliminating Agnew's on the way.

There was a pause. Four times Mr Chance put the price to Mr Simon. 'The bidding is against you at 740,000 guineas,' he said. Mr Simon sat tight, without speaking.

'Going, Going. Gone.' The hammer came down.

It was then that Mr Simon spoke. 'You had the instructions,' he said. 'I have got the letter in my pocket.'

Mr Chance: 'But I said the bidding was against you.'

Mr Simon was on his feet, and adamant. There had been an arrangement, he insisted, that while he was sitting down he was still bidding. And he had not got up once. He insisted, producing the letter from his pocket. It was an agreement he had come to with another Christie's director:

'Lot 105: *Portrait of Titus*.

When Mr Simon is sitting down, he is bidding. If he bids openly when sitting down, he is also bidding.

When he stands up he has stopped bidding. If he then sits down again, he is not bidding until he raises his finger.

Having raised his finger, he is continuing bidding until he stands up again.'

Not surprisingly, Mr Chance thought there was 'some confusion'. In accordance with auction practice, he said, there was a dispute and so the bidding would reopen.

It did. Mr Simon bid 760,000 guineas and amid a great hubbub the lovely little picture was knocked down to him. It took some days and several letters to *The Times* of London before the furore died down.

The buyer, Norton Simon, is one of America's very rich men, and has long been known as a shrewd collector. He made his fortune running a Los Angeles steel corporation and survived the depression with his wealth intact. Subsequently he acquired controlling interest in other companies.

His paintings have been reputed to be worth more than 100 million dollars and in 1971 he sold seventy-three Impressionists at Sotheby–Parke–Bernet for more than six million dollars. He is regarded with some reserve by the English art scene, which likes to place its people in categories, and they are never quite sure how to classify Norton Simon, who does most of his own buying. Collector, connoisseur or dealer, Norton Simon makes very few mistakes.

19. Stubbs' *Goldfinder*, auctioned at Christie's in 1966, made 72,000 guineas ($211,680). Eight years later the painting had tripled in value at Sotheby's.

20. Remington's extraordinary painting *Coming to the Call* was sold by Parke–Bernet in December 1970 for $105,000. It came from the collection of the late Matilda R. Wilson of Rochester, Michigan.

21. So far, the most expensive English painting —Gainsborough's portrait of Mr and Mrs John Gravenor and their daughters, Elizabeth and Dorothea. Sold at Sotheby's on 19 July 1972 for £280,000.

22. The highest auction price paid for a German painting was £224,000—at Sotheby's in 1969, for *The Temptation of Eve*, by Hans Baldung Grien.

23. Dating from 1913, Franz Marc's *Die Blaue Fohlen* fetched $165,000 (£66,000) at Sotheby's.

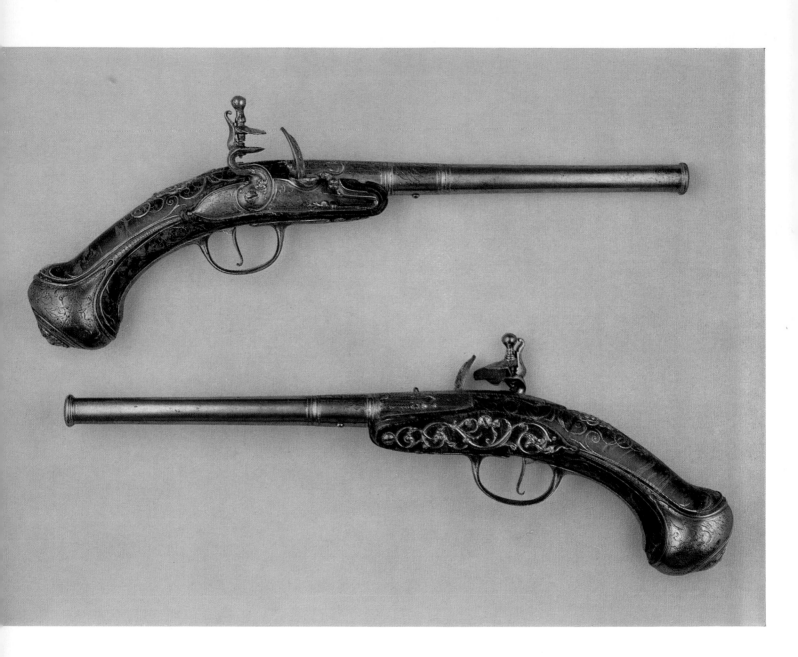

24. Late-seventeenth-century English pistols,
made by a Dutch immigrant gunsmith,
Andrew Dolep. Sale price in 1972, £15,500
($38,750).

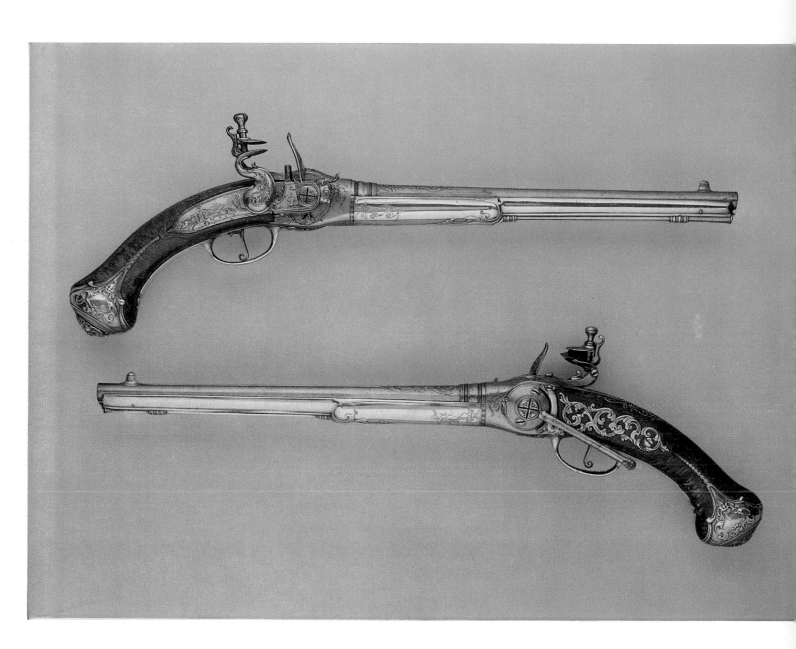

25. The £60,000 ($150,000) flintlock repeating pistols, made by Michele Lorenzoni, gunmaker to the Duke of Tuscany.

26. *Pour une Façade de Musée* was the first Pevsner bronze to appear at auction. It sold for £32,000 ($80,000).

The 'Sixties
Japan Enters the Ring

One of the major features of the London sales seasons of the 'sixties was the increasing interest being taken by Japanese buyers. Indeed, by the early 'seventies, as much as one third of the higher-priced objets d'art and paintings appeared to be finding new homes in the Eastern hemisphere. The movement reflects accurately the growing prosperity of Japan in relation to the Western world, and also the growing appreciation of all forms of art among a public which at one time appeared to Western eyes at least to be formalized and conservative in taste.

Both the major auction houses, who watch trends nearly as closely as they watch each other's activities, have staged sales in Japan; but it was Christie's who made the major breakthrough with the first 'public' auction to be held at the Tokyo Bijutsu Club (a high-class social club) on 27 May 1969. It was an occasion in all senses of the word, and included the Chagall and Rouault paintings shown in colour plates 4 and 5.

(The first and so far the only fully 'public' auction in Japan was held by Sotheby's during British Week in Mitsubishi, Tokyo, six months later, when it was announced that the general public had been allowed to bid for themselves.)

Two months before the sale, the Japanese Ambassador in London was invited to Christie's London salerooms to see the 400-odd items, Impressionist paintings, Western and Oriental porcelain and other items that were shipped to Japan under a heavy security blanket. In fact, it was Christie's name and reputation that probably pushed prices as high as they went, for Japanese collectors had previously suffered from a number of fakes of inferior works that had been foisted on them. This time they got the real thing.

The sale broke new ground in more ways than one. It was the first time a 'public' auction was conducted in Japan—it had always been the custom for dealers only to attend who were members of the club—and the public were able to place their bids through a dealer. Bids were made from London by telephone, but none of them were successful. Custom in Bijutsu Club, which had matted floors throughout, meant that auctioneers, public and dealers alike removed their shoes. Ivan Chance commented to a pressman: 'You can say its the first time I've conducted an auction in my stockinged feet.'

42. Japanese collectors bid high for Modigliani's *Portrait of a Young Farmer*.

The sale totalled over £800,000 (nearly $2,000,000) and many of the prices were higher than they would have been in London or New York. One of the biggest surprises was the Japanese preference for paintings of girls—nudes especially. Even Christie's normally unflappable staff were moved to comment over the hot bidding for a pleasant but unremarkable study of *Seated Girl with a Bowl of Fruit* by the relatively unknown Jules Pascin, which shot up to 14·5 million yen ($40,000); and for a sensuous nude by André Derain which fetched 11 million yen ($30,500).

It was the Japanese taste for the Impressionists and post-Impressionists which really startled the *cognoscenti*. The star item of the collection sold was Modigliani's *Portrait of a Young Farmer* which went for 51 million yen ($141,600) to a dealer on behalf of Taizan Ishibashi, a tyre manufacturer. It was painted in about 1918 and is one of Modigliani's outstanding works. It had been sold at the Parke–Bernet Galleries in New York in 1964 for $60,000. Other examples of astonishing rises included *Portrait of Madame Henriot* by Renoir for 29 million yen ($80,500). This florid work had fetched under $20,000 in London seven years before. A Pierre Bonnard *Young Girl in a Green Dress* made 20 million yen—almost double the price at which it had been withdrawn at a Christie's auction in London a year previously.

In addition, to emphasize the international nature of the occasion a fourteenth-century Chinese Ming vase, which had been handed in for sale by a young Swiss at Christie's office in Geneva, fetched a (then) record auction price of 22 million yen (£26,000; $61,000). It was fifteen inches high, with a design of dragons and flowers.

The 'Seventies
A Cinderella's Millions

The 'sixties went out in a blaze of 'never-to-be-beaten' auction prices, only for the 'seventies to be ushered in by the Dodge Collection sales. It seems almost impossible that the collection was formed in under nine years—between 1930 and the outbreak of the Second World War—and it is a tribute to the energy, taste and the size of the purse of the late Mrs Anna Thomson Dodge that she achieved her remarkable ambition so quickly.

She also achieved other ambitions. For example, she lived to the ripe old age of 103, despite having been burdened for most of her life with riches enough to overwhelm less hardy mortals in half the time. Of all the thousands of rags-to-riches stories that America has produced Mrs Anna Thomson Dodge must have been the most remarkable Cinderella of them all.

Anna landed in America in the 1890s from Dundee, where her father was a penniless sailmaker, with little more than a knowledge of how to teach the piano, an occupation she apparently performed rather well. She moved to Michigan, and there she met and fell in love with a mechanic named Horace Elgin Dodge. When they got married in 1896 Horace had 75 cents in his pocket, so she didn't marry him for his money. The newlyweds spent 45 cents for their honeymoon suite for one night and 20 cents for breakfast. Thus they started married life with 10 cents. Understandably, they moved in with Horace's parents.

Horace was a go-getter. He opened a small bicycle factory with his brother John, and they branched out into making spare parts for Henry Ford. By 1914 they were manufacturing their own Dodge cars. They grew with the rest of the automobile giants to run their own 'stable'—Chrysler, De Soto, Plymouth as well as Dodge itself. And the cash began to accumulate, although it seemed that the very idea of it frightened both the former mechanic and the former piano teacher. David Dodge is quoted as saying that his grandmother wanted to live to be 100 so she could shield her heirs from the 'unbelievable horrors' of estate transfer, 'the money, the power, the corruption, the conniving, the scheming and the intrigue.'

If this may have sounded a little melodramatic, as if Anna and Horace cried all the way to the bank, perhaps the story of one item in her jewellery collection may give some clue to her feelings.

In 1920 Horace won a $40,000,000 court judgement against the Ford Motor Company. To please the little woman who once said her happiest days were those when she packed sandwiches for his lunch, Horace bought her a necklace for $825,000. It consisted of five strands of 389 matched pearls which had once graced the neck of Catherine II of Russia. It was his first and last lavish gift to her; she had worn it only twice when he died seven months later and, stricken with grief, she gave it to her daughter Delphine. Delphine died in 1943 at the age of forty-four, and Mrs Dodge sold—yes, sold—it to Delphine's daughter Yvonne, who borrowed $400,000 from her inheritance to pay for it. It is said that the pearls were delivered by armed uniformed guards who brought them to a private office at a bank. Yvonne simply dropped the pearls, probably worth $2,500,000 at today's prices into her handbag and left. Then she cut the necklace up into more fashionable chokers.

It was the same with the two-million-dollar, 275 ft steam yacht which Horace had built for her. It was finished a year after his death. For a time Anna refused to use it or even to set foot upon it. But when she finally cast off her widow's weeds and emerged, she was good and ready for the biggest single female spending spree on record. First, though, her native Scottish canniness saw to it that she invested the $59,000,000 she inherited from Horace entirely in tax-free bonds issued by municipalities. By this simple but obvious device the merry widow assured herself a yearly income of an average of a million and a half dollars a year for the next fifty years, a low-yield one perhaps, but one that allowed her to emerge unscathed from the Wall Street crash of 1929 and to live the life of the very *grande dame* without dipping into her capital. And she never paid one penny in US Federal tax.

Now, after more than half a century of thrift, she was ready to indulge herself. In 1923 she met an unsuccessful actor, sixteen years younger than she, named Hugh Dillman, who not only taught her to 'have fun with my money' but married her in 1926. He encouraged her to buy a palatial estate in Palm Beach where the happy couple gave parties that became legendary. Dillman might not have been able to act, but he knew how to throw a party. One featured 200 guests, two orchestras, a champagne fountain and 25 lb of Beluga caviare in an ice sculpture.

Above all, Anna Dodge Dillman discovered art—and Lord Duveen, variously described as the art world's super salesman of the time, the doyen of the art dealers, 'that old rogue' and other less complimentary things. Whatever was thought of his dealings however, and some of the published correspondence between him and the Dillmans are masterpieces of the salesman's art, there is no doubt that he was the leading art dealer in the world in the 'twenties and 'thirties and that he exercised much influence on the lady with millions to spend.

It was thanks to, and mainly through, Duveen, that Mrs Dodge Dillman conceived her ruling passion for all things French. With Duveen at her side, she called in French architects, designers and landscape specialists and gave them explicit instructions to build her a French château at her lakeside property at Grosse Pointe in the fashionable outskirts of Detroit. She called it Rose Terrace, and it was to be furnished with the riches that she was starting to collect from all over the world, via Duveen.

She supervized the first three years of the work herself. Then she announced that she was leaving on a world tour on her yacht *Delphine*. During her absence the whole project was to be completed, including a pier ready so that the *Delphine* could be tied up at the water's edge. The grounds were to be landscaped according to her instructions, and Duveen was to scour the world for Beauvais tapestries, Bouchers and Fragonards and as much of Marie Antoinette's furniture as he could lay his hands on. David Dodge recalled: 'She wanted to provide a perfect setting for her furniture. She had a very clear and precise idea of what she wanted and this house was a very true reflection of her understanding of colour and proportion. She fought with the designers over every small detail.'

The high-ceilinged mansion was symmetrical in almost every detail. Its forty-two glass French doors were fourteen feet high, making the château light and airy inside. The wood in the dining room was 400 years old, so that it wouldn't warp after it had been carved. Yet she was remarkably parsimonious in other ways. She wouldn't buy a new television to replace the broken-down set she watched endlessly and eventually one of her grandsons bought her one as a present. She ruled out cutting down a tree because she thought $325 was too expensive and, feeling that she had spoiled her own children (her son Horace married five times and her daughter three), she bestowed few toys on her grandchildren and refused to allow one grandson to have a car before he was twenty-one.

A year after the instructions, in 1936, the *Delphine* steamed into Lake St Clair and Anna was home. The pier was ready, the grounds looked beautiful. Everyone agreed it was a palace fit for Royalty. Lord Duveen was there, clad immaculately in his morning coat, and the assembled company watched as the Queen of the Dodge fortunes stepped ashore. Once the formalities were out of the way, Anna said nothing. Duveen walked with her as she inspected the landscaped gardens dripping with roses. Anna remained silent. The welcoming party bowed her into the main hall. Anna looked around silently and began to ascend the grand staircase. Near the top she turned to Duveen and delivered her verdict: 'This simply won't do!'

It was a remark matching the 'We are not amused' of another more highly-born monarch, but Mrs Dodge managed to turn Rose Terrace into a palace that could be lived in as well as serve as a museum. She began to put on airs and graces appropriate to the mistress of the new Versailles. Servants, her own family and close friends took to calling her 'The Queen'. She didn't discourage them; in fact, she seemed to have entered another century. Those who were closest to her came to believe that Anna, the millionaire's widow, actually regarded herself as a latter-day Marie Antoinette or Madame de Pompadour. At enormous cost she surrounded herself with Marie Antoinette's own furniture (thanks to Duveen); she read everything she could find dealing with France in the eighteenth century, the monarchs and especially the *grande-dames* of the period. She became such an authority that Hollywood studios would send their researchers to her to authenticate props and costumes for films of the Bourbons. In 1932, she commissioned the British artist Sir Gerald Kelly to paint her as Madame de Pompadour for the library at Rose Terrace. For the sitting she had a romantic gown made identical to the one Pompadour wore in the famous portrait of her by Boucher—deep décolletage and a frothing mass of bows. She even had her heroine's jewellery copied.

Anna's second marriage finally ended in divorce in 1947, and she lived on in lonely grandeur at Rose Terrace until, at 103, she died. Like the royalty she emulated, she lay in state for two days at Rose Terrace. Twelve men were required to carry her 2,300-lb bronze coffin; there were sixteen cars full of grieving relatives—the leading limousine was a black Chrysler with a custom built Italian body which she had ordered six years before but had never seen.

On Monday, 27 September 1971, that car, like a thousand other items, became just another number in a catalogue. It was the first great house sale ever mounted in America and Chicago society was there to watch it. The limousines, the maids' beds and the rest fetched £272,328 ($653,587)—not bad when you consider that the *real* goodies had already fetched nearly £2,000,000 ($5,000,000) in London and Geneva.

In spite of her preference of things French, Anna had not restricted herself. She collected jewellery of course, Chinese porcelains, jades and hardstones, English and continental silver and pictures, objets d'art and vertu from all over the world. In spite of her foibles, she had taste and feeling and her wealth enabled her not only to indulge herself but also to protect her property. The collection remained at Rose Terrace until she died.

She bequeathed the contents of the Music Room to the Detroit Institute of Art, which inherited a fine collection of Sèvres porcelain, French furniture and paintings and two fine Gainsborough portraits. Christie's sold the rest.

A selection of pictures, objects of vertu, works of art, French furniture, tapestries, sculptures and metalwork were flown from Detroit and sold in London and Geneva for just under £2,000,000

43, 44, 45. Rose Terrace, the Dodge home on the outskirts of Detroit: exterior, dining room and library.

($4,800,000). Of this sum £382,000 ($916,000) was for Mrs Dodge's jewellery which was sold at the Hotel Richemond in Geneva, (site of the famous Nina Dyer jewel sale).

The works of art sold in London were remarkable for the number of pieces with a royal provenance or connection. A pair of pastoral scenes (colour plates 6 and 7) by the florid French painter François Boucher, *La Fontaine d'Amour* and *La Pipée aux Oiseaux* are traditionally thought to have been painted to the order of Madame de Pompadour to revive the flagging ardours of Louis XV. (As the modern saying goes: It all depends on what turns you on!) At a later date they found their way (as spoils of war?) to Britain and passed from the collection of Lord Tweedmouth to that of Lord Michelham. They hung in the latter's house in Arlington Street, five minutes' walk from Christie's, and were sold in 1926 by the Dowager Lady Michelham. Mrs Dodge acquired them through Lord Duveen and they held pride of place at Rose Terrace until they were flown back for sale. Now, for 400,000 guineas ($1,106,000), the pair found a new home at Mr J. Paul Getty's Museum in California. A delightful set of four rustic scenes by Jean Honoré Fragonard, *The Shepherdess*, *The Grape Gatherer*, *The Reaper* and *The Gardener*, painted for the Duc de Rochechouart for his mansion at Faubourg St Germain in 1753, were bought by the Detroit Institute of Art for 110,000 guineas ($265,000).

The collection contained a number of Royal busts, the most remarkable being a white marble bust of Louis XV by Jean Baptiste Lemoyne;

46, 47. J. H. Fragonard: *The Grape Gatherer* and *The Shepherdess*—two of the four rustic scenes bought by the Detroit Institute of Art.

and it also contained several pieces of seat furniture which had been graced in the centuries gone by by many a Royal posterior. There was the chaise de la Reine bearing the stencil mark of the Garde-Meuble de la Reine Marie Antoinette, the pair of chaises-chauffeuses with the Versailles Palace brand and the Louis XV period pliants, or X-shaped folding stools, one bearing the Tuileries Palace mark.

But the pièce de resistance, for which Christie's really poured the champagne, was Marie-Feodorovna's bureau plat (colour plate 10). This little table, of immaculate taste and impeccable pedigree, sold for more than double the previous world-record auction price for a single piece of furniture. It fetched 165,000 guineas ($415,000), paid by a Lebanese collector, Mr H. Sabet, after a spirited duel with the Detroit Institute of Art.

The bureau plat is mounted with Sèvres plaques bearing the date letter for 1778, and the decoration is probably by the flower-painter Bertrand. The underside bears the trade-label of the marchand-mercier, Dominique Daguerre, which is inscribed: 'Daguerre, Marchand, Rue St Honoré, vis-à-vis l'Hotel d'Aligre. Tient Magazine de Porcelaines, Bronzes, Ebenisterie, Glaces, Curiosités, autre Merchandises, à Paris.'

It is stamped with the initials JME and an obliterated· signature. The experts say, however, that it can be attributed with confidence to the celebrated cabinet-maker Martin Carlin. It was acquired from Daguerre, whose predecessor Poirier is known to have ordered a quantity of porcelain-mounted furniture from Carlin. Their factory had a virtual monopoly to acquire porcelain plaques from the Sèvres factory for mounting on furniture. It is also almost identical, with the exception of the plaques, to a table stamped by Carlin in the Victoria and Albert Museum in London.

The table formerly stood in the bedroom of the Grand Duchess Marie-Feodorovna (later the Czarina of Paul I) at the Palace Pavlovsk in Leningrad, and the Grand Duchess described it in her manuscript notes on her furniture which she complied in 1795 as 'une table longue dont la bord est en porcelaine de Sèvres'.

Half an hour before the bureau plat came under the hammer, a pair of commodes (colour plate 11) made by Bernard Van Risenburgh II produced the very high bid of 80,000 guineas ($200,000). They were of particular interest, because not only was the quality of the marquetry and ormolu superb, but the pair had inter-related motives symbolizing the chase, suggesting that they may have been designed for a royal hunting lodge. The pair was traditionally the property of the Kings of Saxony, having been given by Louis, son of the Grand Dauphin, to the King of Saxony, who was the father of Louis' second wife Marie-Joseph, whom he married in 1747.

The Dodge collection produced a crop of records which provided a springboard for even more remarkable sales to come in the 'seventies.

The 'Seventies
The Million-pound Picture

Of all the great art sales of the twentieth century, none have caused more stir than two held within six months of each other by Christie's. On 27 November 1970, Velasquez's portrait of his mulatto slave, Juan de Pareja (colour plate 8) became known as 'the first million-pound picture', when it fetched £2,310,000; and on 25 June 1971, one of Titian's masterpieces, *The Death of Actaeon* (colour plate 12) was sold for £1,680,000. The importance of the sales, and the furore they caused throughout the art world (and within the more pragmatic walls of the British Treasury) make their stories worth telling in special detail.

Velasquez ranks as one of the world's greatest painters and his works appear very rarely on the art market. *Portrait of Juan de Pareja*, or *Juan* as the masterpiece is familiarly called, is an important and well documented example of Velasquez's work, which dates from around the middle of his career, when he was painter to King Philip IV of Spain. At the time the king was planning a picture gallery, and Velasquez suggested that he should go to Italy himself to buy pictures and sculpture for the king. The king agreed, and Velasquez sailed from Malaga to Genoa in January 1649, taking with him the faithful Juan.

He seems to have had a great shopping spree himself, buying works of his personal favourites among the renaissance masters—Titian, Tintoretto and Veronese, Bassano and Raphael. He eventually reached Rome in July, and there he received a commission to paint the portrait of Pope Innocent X. This portrait, which is now in the Galleria Doria-Pamphili in Rome, is one of his most famous canvases. However, the labours of buying pictures for the king and, no doubt, the joys of long-distance travel in the fifteenth century had left Velasquez's painting arm a little rusty. He needed to practise—a fact which was well described by a near-contemporary historian, Antonio Palomino, writing in 1724.

'When he determined to draw the picture of the Holy Father, he thought to prepare himself beforehand, by way of Exercise, in painting some Head from Life; for which purpose he drew that of Juan de Pareja, (a slave of his and an ingenious Painter) with such Similitude and Liveliness that, having sent it by the same Pareja to some friends to pass their Judgement on it, they stood a while looking sometimes on the Picture and sometimes on the Original, with Amazement and even a sort of Terror, without knowing which they were to speak to, or which was to answer them.'

No one, incidentally, looking at the picture would describe Pareja's features or his demeanour, as painted by Velasquez, as those of a slave. In fact, he was Velasquez's assistant, and himself came to enjoy no small reputation later in Rome. The portrait itself was exhibited in 1650 and was apparently highly acclaimed.

Eventually the portrait found its way to Naples, where it was acquired by the resident British Ambassador, Sir William Hamilton (the husband of Nelson's mistress), himself a great connoisseur and collector, from the Duca di Baranello, and it is included in his manuscript catalogue made at the Palazzo Sessa, Naples, on 14 July 1798, where it appears in the list of pictures in the gallery. But in November of the same year, King Ferdinand of Naples decided to attack the French. As Hamilton had no wish to see his collection fall into French hands, should the King's expedition fail, he gave orders for the Palace to be dismantled.

All the best canvases and drawings were packed under the supervision of James Clark, a picture restorer and minor painter who carefully listed every item in a 'Catalogue of Pictures, Marbles, Bronzes etc., the Property of the Right Honourable Sir William Hamilton K.B. etc., etc. . . Packed at Naples in October, November and December 1798. Under the Direction of Sir William's much obliged and most obedient humble Servant James Clark.'

Number 12 in Case number 7 was described as 'Velasquez Portrait of a Man, Half Figure, Spanish Dress, Height 3 *palme* 1 *once* Breadth 2 *palme* 8 *once*.'

Although Hamilton lost a great part of his collection of antiquities, most of his paintings reached London, having been rescued by Nelson on the *Foudroyant*. Early in 1801 Sir William made arrangements with James Christie to sell some of them, and *Juan* went to an unknown buyer for a niggardly 39 guineas. However, Sir William appears to have been easily satisfied, for he wrote to a friend that Christie had given him in writing the produce of the sale 'with my balance much greater than I thought.' Ten years later it was back at Christie's, where it was bought by the second Earl of Radnor for £151.14s.5d. and remained at Longford Castle until it was sold in 1970 to defray the seventh Earl's death duties.

When Christie's announced the sale, there was immediate uproar. Speculation on the possible price ranged from £200,000 to £1,000,000 with art sales correspondents in British national newspapers raising the question of possible Government intervention to save the picture as part of 'Britain's artistic heritage'. Geraldine Keen, of *The Times*, who fully expected the magic million to be surpassed, explained that under British law, before the painting could leave the country, it had to have an export licence from the Reviewing Committee on the Export of Works of Art. She predicted that the bidding from overseas museums—in particular American museums—would force the bidding to a point where the British Government, always in need of foreign currency, would do nothing to prevent its leaving. Unless the Treasury were to make a massive grant to the National Gallery, the Velasquez would be lost to Britain.

Dr Martin Davis, Director of the National Gallery, said 'it would be a "disaster" if the painting left the country', and Mr Hugh Leggatt, a major London art dealer, was quoted as saying that the sale would be a crucial test of the Government's policy on the arts. 'If this picture does go abroad,' he said, 'it will be not only a tragic loss to our artistic heritage but a national tragedy for our dignity.' The Minister for Arts, Lord Eccles, remained silent.

The sale lasted precisely two minutes and twenty-nine seconds. Of all the excellent accounts written at the time, I prefer Colin Simpson's in the *Sunday Times*, not least for its 'atmosphere' and its glimpse into the workings of Christie's. It is like a glimpse under the bonnet of an expensive car.

'Perhaps the most interesting by-product of the Velasquez sale is the way it marked the end of an era in the salerooms.

'The auctioneers have deliberately created a charisma and a formal ceremonial about their profession in an effort to convince their public that they are not, after all, actually engaged in trade. Recruits to the rostrum are garnered with an eye to their social contacts, and a couple of years' service in the Brigade of Guards is as acceptable as a similar period in the archives of the Uffizi.

'Friday's sale sounded the death-knell of this concept, because it was a triumph for the intellectual midriff of the corporate animal Christie. The painstaking four-page scholarly catalogue entry was the work of David Carrit and William Mostyn-Owen. The bibliography was one of the most detailed ever produced by the firm... Long before the sale was publicly announced, colour transparancies were on the desks of Museum curators throughout the world. When auctioneer Patrick Lindsay opened the sale, the firm was about to discover that not only were they tradesmen again, but very professional tradesmen indeed.

'The price was no surprise to the younger professionals there, but it had shaken some of the senior management to the core. Up to the minute that the Velasquez was introduced, it had been comfortably assumed that the picture might just fetch a million, and that Geoffrey Agnew (London's biggest dealer) would buy it. As the portrait was brought into the saleroom, Agnew's dark green van cruised quietly up to the front door onto the focus marks chalked on the road by a well-briefed TV crew, and two Agnew porters took up their positions in the main hall ready to bear away the main object of the morning's elaborate ritual.

'The first bidder was an anonymous gentleman concealed in a waiting room, and connected to the rostrum by telephone. Hugh Leggatt, a well-known London connoisseur and dealer, quickly despatched him, only to give way to Agnew at £1¼ million. As Agnew bid, Alec Wildenstein capped him, raising the price 100,000 guineas at a time. At £2,100,000 Agnew faltered, and after a brief consultation with his phalanx of directors, tried to break the spiral with an offer of an extra £50,000. Remorselessly Wildenstein capped it, and Agnew conceded.'

Alec Wildenstein is the fourth generation of his family dealing in art. His father, Daniel, is head of the firm, with headquarters in New York. Wildenstein's are probably the richest art dealers in the world. In the vaults of their New York gallery they hold a stock about which myths are woven. Many of the paintings are never shown to the public nor are they for sale. They recently delved into them to fit out the whole museum at Sao Paulo in Brazil and could, apparently, do it all over again.

After the sale, Alec Wildenstein promptly applied for an export licence for the Velasquez, in the buying of which, he said, he had fulfilled his great-grandfather's dream. The old gentleman, Nathan Wildenstein, had seen the painting and vowed that one day Wildenstein's would have it.

Immediately, a 'Save the Velasquez' campaign was mounted in Britain, headed by the National Gallery. The position was that if the Appeal could raise the necessary £2,300,000 to offer Wildenstein's within three months, then the export licence would not be issued. Art lovers brought pressure on the House of Commons to move the Government's stony heart, so accurately predicted by Geraldine Keen.

Lord Eccles, the Minister for the Arts, commented sourly that the amount needed was 'very large' and muttered vaguely about finding a 'wealthy benefactor'. *The Times* came out strongly against taxpayers' money being used; the picture, it said, would be a doubtful case at half the price. The art world, it said, had over-reached itself this time. And *The Guardian* pointed out caustically that 'if *Juan* belonged to anyone's national heritage, it was that of Spain'.

In the event, all the huffing and puffing was in vain. *Juan* went off to fulfil a Wildenstein dream, and is now in the Metropolitan Museum, New York.

(Incidentally, although *Juan* made the highest figure recorded at a public auction, the highest price ever paid for a picture was £4,220,000, paid by the Washington National Gallery for Leonardo da Vinci's *Ginevra dei Benci* in a private deal with the royal family of Liechtenstein some years before.)

No sooner had the ripples left behind by *Juan* died down, than the never peaceful surface of the art world in Britain was shaken by the announcement that the Earl of Harewood had decided to withdraw Titian's masterpiece, *The Death of Actaeon* (colour plate 12) from the National Gallery, where it had been on loan for ten years, and sell it. Probably because it had been on public view, whereas *Juan* had been tucked away in the country at Longford Castle, the furore was even greater.

Actaeon is a *big* picture—in every sense of the word. It measures 70½ in. high by 78 in. across, and it shows the hunter, Actaeon, fleeing from a rather muscular Diana, Goddess of Hunting, whom he had disturbed while she was bathing with her attendants. Diana is seen shooting an arrow into Actaeon, which turns him into a stag, to be devoured by her dogs.

It is thought that Titian must have been at least seventy when he painted *The Death of Actaeon* for he refers to it in a letter sent to King Philip of Spain in 1559. Titian (1488–1576) is generally considered to be the greatest of all the Venetian painters and connoisseurs through the years have generally agreed that his own hopes were fulfilled. 'I shall put into this all the knowledge that God has given me', he told Philip. And certainly the eulogies of praise, both fulsome and sincere, written since would fill many volumes.

This time the sale took a mere ninety seconds. It was conducted by Mr Chance and in next to no time at all *Actaeon* had been knocked down for a mere 1,600,000 guineas to an American dealer, Mr Julius Weitzner. The triumphant American was promptly surrounded by photographers and reporters, but he forced his way through them and fled, hotly pursued, round the corner into a fine-art gallery in Duke Street. Before she shut the door in their faces, his daughter, Marjorie, told the reporters that Daddy had bought the painting for her, because it would fit perfectly well above her fireplace, but no one took that seriously.

Mr Weitzner had come into the news some three years before when he bought a Duccio *Madonna and Child with Angels* at a Somerset auction for £2,700 and re-sold it to the National Gallery for a trifling £150,000.

After the *Actaeon* sale he was quoted as saying he didn't know why the bidding was so low—he expected to have had to have paid more for the picture. At any rate, the storm which now broke over the unfortunate head of Lord Eccles made the previous rumpus over the Velasquez look like an April shower. And it blew into a hurricane when, three days later, Mr Weitzner announced that he'd sold the painting to the Getty Museum in Malibu, California for a 'nominal' profit. It turned out later that 'nominal' meant around £80,000, which wasn't bad for three days' work.

In fact, Mr Weitzner had been perfectly correct in his estimate of the situation. The 'under-bidder', that is the bidder who finally dropped out, had been representing the Getty Museum, and had wisely calculated that they could save a great deal of cash by 'losing' the public auction and doing a private deal. As the bids were lifting at the rate of a hundred thousand guineas a time, Mr Weitzner's profit represented less than one bid, and in such relative terms 'nominal' doesn't seem too bad a word.

However, this time the Government *did* step in. Lord Eccles announced a little while later that the Government was not prepared to grant an exit licence for *Actaeon* for the time being, in order to allow the National Gallery to raise the £1,763,000 to buy the painting for Britain. The National Gallery pledged all the money allowed to them that year—£400,000 and then raised another £600,000 by persuading the Government to advance them £150,000 from each of their next four year's grants, making a total of £1 million. Then the Government made a remarkable and imaginative offer. A sum of £763,000 was still needed, and the Government would match all public subscriptions until the sum was reached—in effect a special grant of £381,500. The National Arts Collections Fund offered £100,000 and the Pilgrim Trust £50,000; Weitzner himself donated £1,000 to the fund. On 6 July 1972 the National Gallery Trustees handed over the full cheque for £1,763,000.

If, however, you come to the conclusion from all this that the British Government had suddenly found a soul in relation to Great Master paintings, there were still plenty of sceptics to point out that of the original price, something like seventy per cent would have returned to them in direct taxation, and presumably they would also have taken a fair bite out of Mr Weitzner's £80,000.

But that was of no concern to Christie's, who had conducted another record sale. In fact, the overall sale of twenty-seven lots broke every record for an art auction and may never be reached again (although such predictions in the art world are presumptuous). Another masterpiece, Van Dyck's famous study of *Four Negro Heads* (colour plate 14) sent in by Lord Derby, was bought by the American dealers, French and Co. for £400,000 ($1,000,000), ten times more than any painting by Van Dyck had ever fetched before. It had been sent in by Lord Derby from the Walker Gallery in Liverpool, where it had been on view for many years.

The 'Seventies
The New York Jungle

By the end of the 1971–2 season, the annual turnover of the Sotheby–Parke–Bernet combination had risen to £43 millions (over $100,000,000) a year, and the sales, both in London and New York, were reaching new heights. Perhaps the most outstanding were the Impressionist, post-Impressionist and modern sales, particularly in New York, where Henri Rousseau's *Paysage Exotique* was bought by the Norton Simon Foundation for $775,000 (£310,000). It was the highest price for any twentieth-century work of art. The subject of the jungle fascinated Rousseau, and of the large number of compositions he executed this is generally regarded to be one of the finest. It was painted in 1910, the year Rousseau died.

There was an enormous demand for German Expressionist paintings, and the sale by the Solomon R. Guggenheim Foundation of forty-eight oils and watercolours by Kandinsky for a total of $1,995,500 (£782,200) was the most important event. This sale included *Bild mit drei Flecken Nr 196* of 1914, which realized a world record of $300,000 (£120,000) for the artist's work. When the Guggenheim Foundation sold another superb group of fifty paintings by Kandinsky at Sotheby's in 1963, the total was £536,500 ($1,502,200)—but this was for the forty-nine oils and one gouache. The 1971 sale was of fifteen oils only.

Another very rare piece was the composition by Franz Marc *Die blaue Fohlen* of 1913 (colour plate 23). Marc was a seminal figure, with Kandinsky, in founding the Blue Rider group and because of his early death in the First World War his mature work is seldom on the market. It fetched $165,000 (£66,000).

Four exceptional sculptures came under the Sotheby hammer during the season—all of them for record prices. Possibly the most important of all the sales was at Parke–Bernet in March, when Barlach's wood carving of 1911, *Der Schweitzer*, fetched $110,000 (£44,000) and, even more impressive, Henry Moore's monumental elmwood *Reclining Figure* realized $260,000 (£104,000). This sculpture has inspired more criticism and analysis than almost any other contemporary piece since its creation in 1945–6. Moore has described his feelings when he was carving both this one for the Cranbrook Academy of Arts, Bloomfield Hills, Michigan, and the Dartington Hall *Reclining Figure*.

'For Dartington Hall I chose an idea which was calm and peaceful and seemed to me to be most suitable. But at the same time, in my studio, I was doing a large wood sculpture which was very different in spirit. This was at a time when I was catching up on the two years of sculpture time I had lost through the war and I had many accumulated ideas to get rid of. And so I was doing two sculptures at the same time although the two were completely different from each other in mood. Thus I was able to satisfy both sides of my nature by working on the rather gentle Dartington figure at the same time as the Cranbrook *Reclining Figure* in Elmwood, which for me had great drama, with its big beating heart like a great pumping station.'

Anton Pevsner's *Pour une Façade de Musée* (see colour plate 26) was the first bronze by this artist to appear at auction, and, not surprisingly it fetched £32,000 ($80,000) in London in May. The next month, a Modigliani stone head (colour plate 15) executed around 1910 fetched the surprising figure of £72,000 ($180,000). This sculpture had been known only from a photograph taken in 1911, and the reappearance of the work after more than sixty years produced a valuable addition to the twenty-five sculptures which were all that was thought to have survived.

Sotheby's stole the jewellery limelight during the season with two events at Zurich which between them realized £1,971,407 ($4,928,519). The outstanding piece of jewellery was a necklace in emeralds and diamonds, most of which at one time had been part of a necklace owned by Tsar Alexander II of Russia. This fetched 4,300,000 Swiss Francs, or £436,550. In sterling this was second only to the £437,500 paid in New York by Richard Burton for the famous Winston diamond in 1969 for Elizabeth Taylor, but because of the vagaries of international exchange the necklace actually made more dollars (1,091,370 compared with 1,050,000 for the Burton diamond).

The top American sale of 1971 was undoubtedly part of Mr Norton Simon's collection at Sotheby–Parke–Bernet on 5 May. Superb paintings by Boudin, Van Gogh, Degas, Monet and Signac all fetched exceptional prices, whilst Degas' magnificent bronze *Petite Danseuse de Quartorze Ans*, unquestionably one of the greatest sculptures of the nineteenth century, realized $380,000, the highest sum yet paid at auction for a sculpture of any period. The last cast of this piece fetched $30,000 at Parke–Bernet in 1955.

Boudin's *Crinolines sur la Plage*, which measures only 14 in. by $22\frac{3}{4}$ in., fetched $160,000. Van Gogh's *L'Hôpital de St Paul à Saint-Rémy* reached a staggering $1,200,000, while Renoir's voluptuous *La Source* made $230,000. Gauguin's self-portrait added another $420,000 to the total and Monet's *Le Bassin de Nympheas, Giverny*, fetched $320,000.

The 'Seventies
Stubbs and the 'Tyger'

On 30 June 1764, the Duke of Cumberland conducted a hunting experiment in Windsor Great Park which would have greatly perturbed the animal lovers of today. The whole affair was described in the current issue of the *Gentleman's Magazine*. The noble duke had loosed 'one of His Highness's tygers' on to an English stag.

'The tyger attempted to seize the stag, but was beat off by the horns; he made a second attack at the throat, and the stag tossed him an astonishing height; a third time the tyger attempted to seize him, but the stag threw him as before and then followed him. The tyger faced him no more, but ran under the toils and pursued a herd of deer, one of which he instantly killed; but while he was devouring a part of him, two Indians that followed him, threw a kind of hood over his head, and then fastened a chain about his neck, let him fill his belly and led him quietly to his den.'

From contemporary evidence, laid out in scholarly fashion in Sotheby's *Art at Auction* (1969–70) by Basil Taylor, it appears quite likely that the 'tyger' was in fact a cheetah that had been presented to King George III by one George Pigot, Governor of Madras from 1755 to 1764, during India's most turbulent period. It also appears likely that Pigot commissioned the famous British artist George Stubbs to place the event on canvas for the princely sum of £120.

He could afford it. He paid £100,000 for his house in Staffordshire, Patshull, and it was rumoured that on his retirement from Madras he received a gift of £40,000 from the Nawab of Arcot. He owned an important diamond, sufficiently famous to bear his name, which he sold in 1818 for £30,000. Duty in India, it seems, was not all hard labour. At any rate, whether for his services in India, his princely gift, or because his mother had been tirewoman (dresser) to the King's grandmother, Caroline of Brunswick, Pigot was granted a baronetcy. Two years later he was granted an Irish peerage, becoming Lord Pigot of Patshull. In 1775 he returned to Fort St George in Madras for a second term, dying there two years later in mysterious circumstances as a prisoner of his own Council.

The artist, Stubbs, was at the peak of his powers at the time, being in his forties. He had come to London in 1760 and immediately estab-

48.   Stubbs' *Tyger*—we know it as a cheetah.

lished a flourishing practice as a painter of animal and sporting subjects. During the decade he won the support of notable sportsmen and politicians; among them the Dukes of Grafton, Portland and Richmond, the Marquis of Rockingham, Viscount Torrington, the Earl of Grosvenor and Lord Bolingbroke.

The expert, Basil Taylor, describes the cheetah painting as the most ambitious of all Stubbs' wild-animal paintings, except perhaps for the largest version which shows a lion attacking a horse.

'As so often, Stubbs had combined the attributes of a noble and formal design with the closest attention to particularities. Here is the cheetah marvellously presented in all its physical power, energy and grace. It wears the accoutrements of a creature trained for hunting, the hood used to cover its eyes and the sash by which it could be held before release. Here are the Indian servants who manage it, rendered without a trace of superstition or European condescension; they are among his finest portraits. The landscape has a slightly exotic appearance, as well as being constructed with a sufficient largeness of design to contain the monumental group in its centre. . . It had no precedent in the history of English Art. . .'

After such an eulogy it is perhaps an anticlimax to record that on 18 March 1970 George Stubbs' *A Cheetah with Two Indians* was bought by the Manchester City Art Gallery for £220,000, at the time a world record for a painting by an English artist.

Five years before, another Stubbs, the magnificent study of *Goldfinder* (see colour plate 19), a champion racehorse, painted in 1774, had been sold at Christie's for 72,000 guineas. Christie's went to some trouble to establish the pedigree of the horse as well as the picture. Goldfinder was traced right back to the 'Darley Arabian' through his dam; and his sire, 'Snap' (whose picture, also by Stubbs, was also sold at the same sale), through *his* dam to the 'Byerly Turk'. These two horses were among the pure Arab stallions imported in Stuart times from North Africa and which formed the taproots of the *British Thoroughbred Stud Book*.

In 1973 *Goldfinder* turned up again—this time in one of the most controversial sales of the century—at Sotheby's. Jack Dick, an American cattle magnate, had been forced to sell because of his debts, including large sums to the United States Internal Revenue Department. With the US Government standing by, Mr Dick's collection of sporting pictures, nearly all of them English, fetched over £1,240,000. *Goldfinder* had more than tripled in value, going for £225,000.

Afterwards Mr Dick said to Peter Wilson, Sotheby's chairman: 'Peter, that was beautiful.'

The 'Seventies
The $500,000 Umbrella Stand

The story of 'The Most Expensive Pot in the World' (colour plate 16) actually began 600 years ago in a kiln in China; but for Anthony Derham, Christie's Director of Oriental Works of Art, it started on a dull winter's day in 1970 when he was performing a routine job—a revaluation for insurance of a private collection in Europe.

On his way out, job completed, he noticed a blue and white jar being used as an umbrella stand in the hall and recognized it as the third only known example of a group of audaciously experimental works from the mid-fourteenth century, the other two being in Peking and in the Percival David Foundation in London.

By 1350, porcelain, as a material, held few secrets from the kiln masters at Ching-te-chen; very large or elaborately potted pieces were made, and the group into which this wine-jar falls is believed to have been the work of one of the most daring kilns. The technicalities involved luting together a heavy slab base, a two-part body thick enough to have panels cut into it during the 'leather' hardness stage, and a short neck; then sticking small pre-moulded flowers and leaves on short stalks into the recessed panels and finally adding double surrounds of 'sugar-icing' beading. To succeed in all these processes was extraordinary enough, but in addition, throughout a long firing serious fluctuation in temperature (controlled by 'draught doors') could cause total collapse and would certainly affect the colour of the underglaze copper-red flowers or the cobalt-blue decoration.

So it was hardly surprising that such a rare and desirable piece of porcelain should achieve a world-record price. Even so, the bid of 210,000 guineas ($573,000)—more than had ever been paid before for any work of art other than a painting—brought loud applause.

Bidding had started at £30,000. The main battle was between John Sparks, London dealers, and Hirano of Osaka. At £200,000 Hirano stopped, but from the back came another Japanese bid and the jar was knocked down to a smiling Mr Sakomoto, whose clients include many of Japan's leading collectors.

Mr Derham said afterwards: 'The owner showed it to me while swinging it with one hand—I nearly collapsed. I knew what it was straight away. During its life as an umbrella stand it survived being handled by the four children of the family. It was damaged earlier. There is a chip on the neck. But it's still better than the other two.'

The 'Seventies
The Dolep Pistols

On 15 May 1972, Sotheby's offered for sale an historic pair of English pistols from the late seventeenth century (colour plate 24). They were made by a Dutch immigrant gunsmith, Andrew Dolep, who was first recorded as working in London in 1681.

The London Gunmakers' Company at first refused him admittance, but eventually, in 1686, he was allowed to join, thanks to the patronage of the Earl of Dartmouth, Master General of the Ordnance. His works are exhibited at Windsor Castle in England, at the Dresden Armoury of the former Kings of Poland and Electors of Saxony, and elsewhere. In 1709 he was appointed to appraise the firearms of Prince George of Denmark, consort of Queen Anne, who had died the previous year. The guns in the Windsor Armoury by Dolep presumably formed part of Prince George's collection.

The pair of pistols sold by Sotheby's for £15,500 ($38,750) is believed to have been a gift from an English King, either Charles II or William III, to the Grand Duke Cosimo III of Tuscany. They were of particular interest to Mr John Hayward, an associate director of Sotheby's, who had made a special study of Dolep's works.

In 1948 Mr Hayward had been invited to report on the collection of arms and armour in the Royal Palace at Turin which had, after the end of the monarchy in Italy, become state property. Among the pieces he identified was an unusual flintlock fowling piece by Andrew Dolep. The gun bears, inlaid on each side of the butt, the monogram F.M. surmounted by the crown of the Grand Dukes of Tuscany, probably for Fernandino de Medici, eldest son of Grand Duke Cosimo III.

Some years later Mr Hayward was in Naples to reorganize and catalogue the arms and armour collection of the former Bourbon kings of the Two Sicilies. There he discovered a pair of pocket pistols of superb quality, also signed by Dolep and bearing the Medici arms. Subsequently, a small combination tool for firearms with the same signature and coat of arms was presented to the Royal Armouries in the Tower of London.

The obvious conclusion was that these arms must have formed part of a set which had been commissioned either by Charles II or William III for presentation to Cosimo. Alternatively Cosimo, who visited England in 1669, may have ordered them himself.

49. The magnificent garniture of French
Empire flintlock firearms by Boutet, sold in
1970 for £43,000 ($103,320).

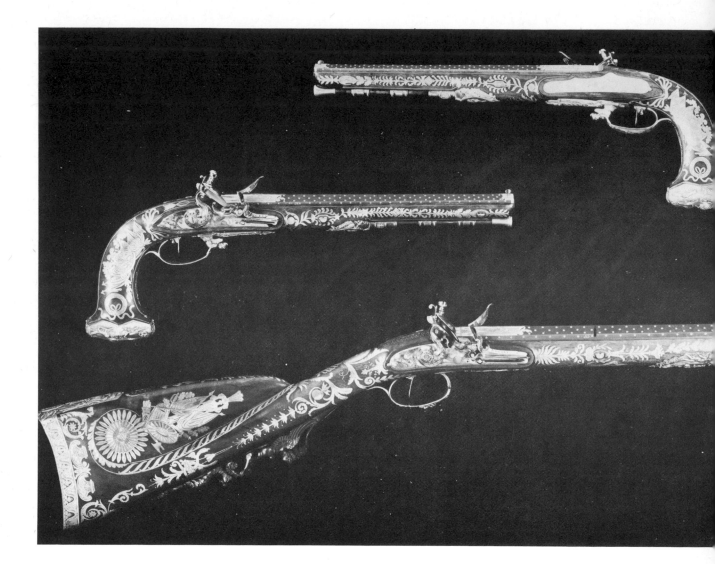

In any case, it was a nice example of historical detection, and Mr Hayward lived in hopes that it would lead to still further discoveries. He wrote in his book *The Art of the Gunmaker*, published in 1963: 'The set was probably completed with a pair of holster pistols as well, which may yet be discovered in some public or private collection.'

Nine years afterwards, the Cranbrook Academy of Arts in Michigan sent along the pistols, well worthy of being a royal gift, to Sotheby's for auction.

The price paid, however, was not the highest reached for a pair of pistols that year. That was £60,000 ($150,000), paid for a pair of flintlock breech-loading repeating pistols with engraved silver mounts and redwood stocks (colour plate 25). They were by Michele Lorenzoni, gunmaker to the Grand Duke of Tuscany. They came from the sale of the collection of the late William Goodwin Renwick of Arizona, and had formerly been in the Imperial Russian collection. This sale broke all records for its field, realizing the huge total of £217,410 ($543,525) for only thirty-eight lots.

A pair of presentation pistols by Nicholas Noel Boutet (also from the Renwick Collection) fetched £19,000 ($47,500). They are believed to have belonged to Napoleon (the butts are inlaid with the Insignia of the Grand Cross of the Légion d'Honneur) and to have been captured during his retreat from Moscow. They then passed into the Imperial Russian Collection, formerly in the Palace of Tsarskoe Seloe, St Petersburg.

Another production of Boutet, catalogued lavishly as a 'garniture of flintlocks', held the record price for any single lot of firearms until the Renwick sale. It was auctioned by Christie's in London in 1970 for £43,500 ($103,320). It formerly belonged to the family of Osten-Stacken, a member of which was Military Governor in Paris in 1814. The garniture comprises a rifle and a pair of pistols, each profusely inlaid with silver and with barrels set with gold stars, accompanied by their full accessories for loading and cleaning, set into the light-blue velvet lining of the veneered mahogany case.

The 'Seventies
Lady Blunt's Violin

This violin (colour plate 17) is believed to be one of three most beautiful in the world. So far, it certainly is the most expensive, for it was sold at Sotheby's on 3 July 1971 for £84,000 ($201,600).

It was made by Antonio Stradivari at Cremona in 1721, the centre of his 'golden period' when he raised violin making to an art which has never since been surpassed. It is in remarkably fine condition, and still bears the original label inscribed: '*Antonius Stradivarius faciebat Cremonensis Anno 1721*'.

The number of Stradivarius violins still remaining is remarkably large (there are over 500 known genuine instruments as well as innumerable fakes) for the old man worked until the year of his death, 1737, when he was ninety-four. His life is generally divided into four periods. In the first, up to about 1690, known as the Amati period, his instruments still bore the influence of his teacher Nicholas Amati and it was only during the last decade of the seventeenth century that his own particular style was evolved. His finest instruments were made between 1715 and 1725. The superiority of Stradivari's instruments does not lie in any one feature but in the combination of finely chosen woods, worked and assembled by a man who was both a brilliant craftsman and an artist. The formula for his beautiful varnishes has been lost, but was probably similar to that of other contemporary Cremonese makers. Although a contributory factor, it is not the secret of the Stradivari tone, which was recognized from the time he made the instruments. As result of their perfection, many Stradivari violins have seen much use and show signs of wear.

The Lady Blunt violin can be counted as among the two or three most important Stradivaris in existence today. Besides its fine tonal qualities, it is in superb condition. It still retains much of the original varnish, except for some early wear on the right of the tail piece, while the edges are as sharp as they were when made. Even the black lines with which Stradivari picked out the edges of the scroll are intact. The violin bears the initials P.S. in ink on the mortice at the base of the pegbox and is believed to be one of the instruments left by Stradivari, on his death, to his third son, Paul.

The violin's history is unknown from 1740 until it was discovered in Spain by the famous French violin maker and dealer J. P. Vuillaume. He adapted the neck and replaced the fingerboard and bass bar to suit modern requirements, but sensibly retained the originals, which still accompany the instrument.

In 1864 Vuillaume sold the violin to Lady Anne Blunt, the granddaughter of Lord Byron and a remarkable traveller, linguist and musician. It remained in her possession until 1895 and since then has been in several important private collections. It was sold at Sotheby's to Sam Bloomfield, a well-known patron of music and himself an amateur musician, from California.

50.   The Butch Cassidy bicycle.

The 'Seventies
Star Dust: at a Price!

Sotheby–Parke–Bernet, Los Angeles came into being in 1970 when the firm bought a real estate 'white elephant' on Beverly Boulevard—a massive building with 12-inch thick concrete walls that had belonged to the American Institute of Aeronautics and Astronautics.

Its first sale was held in February 1971 for 20th-Century Fox, when an amazing collection of film properties and *memorabilia* came under the hammer. Edward J. Landrigen III recalls in *Art at Auction* that the staff soon grew accustomed to the strange consignment and cataloguing went on apace. To combine 38-ft models of the Japanese Navy (*Tora! Tora! Tora!*), the bicycle from *Butch Cassidy and the Sundance Kid*, Shirley Temple's Teddy Bear from *Captain January*, stage coaches, fire-engines and stuffed apes was a challenging task.

The first evening was like a Fox movie première. As the firstcomers arrived the gravel in the front garden was still being levelled. The newly-painted (Sotheby's traditional green) saleroom attracted a bevy of stars such as Debbie Reynolds, David Hemmings, Raymond Massey, Zsa Zsa Gabor, Cornel Wilde, Natalie Wood and Hugh O'Brien. Sotheby's staff were pleasantly surprised to find most of the items in keeping with their estimates, although there were some exceptions.

One was the Butch Cassidy bicycle. Composer Burt Bacharach (*Raindrops are falling on My Head*) was bidding against producers Bert Rosin and David Winters who wanted to present the bike to Joanne Woodward, Paul Newman's wife. Rosin and Winters won the battle, but only after paying $3,100 and bringing the crowd to its feet cheering on the enthusiastic bidders. Raymond Massey bid on a portrait of himself. He lost it at $165 to a news writer who was heavily booed for his pains by the pro-Massey audience. The Massey fans gave the actor a full minute of applause when he rose to leave. A reporter asked Massey why he wanted the portrait, and the actor replied that he felt it was such a dreadful picture he had hoped to take it home and burn it.

The large model ships did well considering the difficulty they offered for portage. Most of them went to maritime museums and shopping centres. Eleven American Navy training aeroplanes, converted to look like Japanese Zeroes, Vals and Zekes for *Tora! Tora! Tora!* fetched an average of $2,350 each from private collectors.

The total for the auction was over $364,000.

Dreams . . .

This chapter is strictly for optimists. If, like me, you've always believed that there *were* fairies at the bottom of the garden (if only you could see them), that the ship will come home or that there really is a crock of gold at the foot of every rainbow, then you'll enjoy it. For the tales are all true.

Arthur Davey is a round-faced, jolly man of about forty. He is a farm labourer, and lives with his wife Margaret in a thatched cottage of ancient stone in the tiny village of Rattlesden, near Stowmarket, Suffolk. He has brought up his family of five on a wage which only in the past few years has reached £18 ($45) a week.

One day in 1972 Arthur was hoeing a row of beet at the farm when his hoe struck something metallic. He thought it was a stone, but something made him examine it more closely. It was a little bronze and silver-gilt statuette (colour plate 18), not quite four inches high, buried there in the mud at his feet. 'I gave it a wipe on the back of my trousers and then just dropped it down at the end of the row,' said Arthur later. 'I didn't think much about it.'

But he picked it up at knocking-off time and took it home, for he's always been a collector of bric-à-brac—'I'm a great one for collecting bits and pieces—old coins and suchlike.'

Margaret was cross. She said she was sick and tired of junk, and if it was left where she could see it, she'd chuck it in the dustbin.

The little figure knocked around the Davey household for a bit after that, but it just wouldn't get lost. Their small daughter, Susan, put it with her dolls for a while, and young Neil tried to swop it for a car with a friend at school. But the friend only had a tractor to exchange, and so Neil stuck it in the glove compartment of Arthur's old car. Eventually, Arthur happened to show it to his brother-in-law's employer, a local farmer who knew a bit about antiques, who persuaded him to take it along to Christie's.

They said it had originally come from a church in France, and dated it back to about 1180. It was a gilt bronze figure of St John the Evangelist. The experts reckoned that it had been stolen centuries ago from nearby Bury St Edmunds, and when the thief realized it wasn't gold or silver, he'd thrown it away in disgust.

On the day Christie's sold it—for £36,750 (nearly $90,000)—Arthur went up to London. He seemed in a bit of a daze and, although Christie's staff were ready with a bottle of champagne, they had to go across to the pub to get him a bottle of light ale. He had one, then another, and then he left without fuss to take a look at the sides of beef at the Smithfield annual show at Earls Court exhibition centre. Then it was back to the farm and an unchanged life—apart from the purchase of a new car and a washing machine.

*

Between them, Christie's and Sotheby's examine more than half a million works of art of one form or another during a year, at least two thirds of which are eventually sold for under £100 each. But some of the ugly ducklings turn out to be swans. Take Mrs Finch's teapot.

Mrs Finch was an old lady from the Isle of Wight. One day she turned up at the front counter with a teapot which, she said, hard times had forced her to try to sell. Her grandmother had used it daily for years; so had her mother, and so had she. She asked Mr Arthur Grimwade if she'd get £20 for it.

'You'll certainly get that for it,' said Mr Grimwade. 'You may even be able to buy a car, provided you don't want a Rolls Royce.'

In fact, when it came up for sale it fetched £1,800. A few years later the new owner offered it again for sale, but bought it in when the bidding reached £4,800.

It was an almost unique seven-sided teapot, made by a famous Huguenot silversmith, Isaac Ribouleau.

51. Mrs Finch's teapot—a mere £1,800!

An old man took a small picture on a board into Sotheby's. 'Is this worth a fiver?' he asked.

One of the directors, who happened to be passing, took a quick look and said: 'Good heavens, sir, you have an early Samuel Palmer there.'

'I know it's a Samuel Palmer,' said the old man. 'He gave it to my grandmother. But is it worth a fiver?'

It sold for £5,600.

*

When the Germans overran Jersey during the last war, Lord Trent's cook threw the family silver down the well in an effort to keep it safe.

Six years later, when the Germans had left, he retrieved it, and when the family got back to Jersey it was all in place in the house again.

Among the silver was a pair of Paul de Lamerie silver-gilt wall sconces which sold at Sotheby's for £23,000.

*

A middle-aged woman who was moving house asked Sotheby's to value her furniture. The furniture expert went down, selected six Chippendale chairs and was about to leave the house when she said, 'Would you mind looking at my picture. I've been told it's a Richard Wilson and is worth up to £200.'

The Sotheby's man said that although he wasn't a picture expert it looked good to him, and advised her to take it up to London. At Sotheby's it was found to be *The Judgement of Paris*, by Claude Lorraine, missing since a sale in Paris in 1724.

It sold for £175,000.

*

Peter Croft, a manuscript expert at Sotheby's, was examining a note-book filled with roughly scribbled notes when he noticed the line 'gather ye rosebuds while ye may.'

He remembered that he had once seen the handwriting of Robert Herrick, the poet, and that the line was, of course, from the famous Herrick poem.

He compared the handwriting in the notebook with the Herrick letters in the Leicester Record Office and it was proved beyond doubt that this was the 'Commonplace' book of the poet. It sold for £34,000.

*

Another book expert, while sorting through a whole room filled with 'rubbish' destined for the pulp merchants, came across a single sheet of ancient writing. He put it on one side as 'interesting' and worth a look at later.

During the day he found many other sheets. When they were examined closely they were found to be the long-lost six chapters of Caxton's translation of Ovid, in the great printer's own hand.

The manuscript sold at Sotheby's for £94,000.

*

One day the wife of a London oil executive brought a picture to Christie's front counter. Her daily help had been clearing out a relation's cottage and had found it among junk ready for burning. Being of a thrifty nature, and having seen her employer's husband repairing furniture in his spare time, she thought he might find some use for 'a nice piece of mahogany'.

When any work of art is accepted by a fine art saleroom it is given a stock number and brief details are written on a receipt form. In this case it was: 'One unframed picture, panel cracked, owner to be advised.' The panel was duly stencilled on the back with its allotted number and put aside for examination.

William Mostyn-Owen, one of Christie's Old Master directors, came across it in due course. He saw that beneath the grime and cracked varnish was a house that could be of some architectural interest. Just visible also was a flag flying from the roof, something like the Tricolour. It wasn't French, but might have been Dutch, and there was a curious carriage, or sledge, coming up the drive from the left. Could it be a troika, and so the Dutch Embassy in Russia? Or perhaps more likely some important Russian official in Holland, grand enough to sport his own troika?

Mostyn-Owen made a careful search with a headlamp. He found a signature: 'A. Schelfhout', and made a note on the manuscript of the catalogue: 'Important to find out what château this is—perhaps Soestdijk, the Dutch Royal Family's palace in the country.'

Count Alexis Bobrinskoy, adviser on Russian works of art, was called in. He recalled that Anna Pavlovna, daughter of Emperor Paul I of Russia, had married King William of Holland and that she had brought a troika with her as a souvenir of her native Russia. In all likelihood this was Queen Anna Pavlovna herself.

A letter and photograph were sent to the Hague, and the reply not only confirmed this possibility, but identified the house as Het Loo, another of the Dutch Royal palaces.

The owners were informed, a reserve price agreed, and the picture put up for sale. The price fetched was 460 guineas—not a very large sum indeed, but 460 guineas more than the piece of mahogany would have fetched on the bonfire or even as a furniture repair. Without the correct historical identification it would not have raised 50 guineas because of its poor condition.

*

It was a good thing that Anthony du Boulay, Christie's porcelain director, enjoyed a game of tennis. He was staying with friends in Yorkshire and was offered the use of a neighbour's court. As he was passing the dining room window, du Boulay spotted a Chinese porcelain flask sitting forlornly beneath a sideboard. It might have been

52. The Ming jar discovered by Anthony du Boulay.

an eighteenth-century copy of little interest, but du Boulay thought, even at thirty feet, that it might be worth a closer look. The maid, he learnt, complained that it got in the way of the vacuum cleaner.

The flask belonged to a rare group of fifteenth-century Ming porcelains, decorated with a dragon in white on a blue background. It had not been documented before and was one of only three such flasks that are known throughout the world, the others being in the Percival David collection in London and in the Peking Museum. In all likelihood it was taken to Britain following the toil of the Boxer Risings in China at the turn of the century.

When it came up for sale, it made £25,200.

*

John Floyd, then Christie's Furniture Director, was searching through a mass of furniture in an attic when he came upon a hat-box. In it was a superb Cartel clock, by Etienne Le Noir, unrecognized, unappreciated as one of the finest examples of Louis XV ormolu works in the world. Not surprisingly, it made a world record auction price of £29,400, which stood until 13 December 1974, when a Lady Baillie Louis XV mantel clock in Chinese porcelain, red lacquer and ormolu, signed Balthazard à Paris fetched £38,000.

53. Mr Peter Wilson, Chairman of Sotheby's.

Mr Wilson of Sotheby's

The mid-century revolution in sales of art—in fact the 'watershed' which set the tone and the scale (and the market values) of the British art market for decades to come—was undoubtedly the great Goldschmidt sale at Sotheby's in 1958. It was a once-in-a-lifetime coup that established not only the British predominance in art sales expertise but also the reputation of the tall thin man who had only recently become chairman of Sotheby's—Peter Wilson.

In appearance and manner Peter Wilson is deceptively quiet and modest. It is hard to believe that this is one of the very few British businessmen who is not only respected but actively feared in the competitive spheres of American business.

'The thing about the Goldschmidt sale', he told me, sitting in the tiny unpretentious 'waiting room' at Sotheby's, 'was that before it, no work of art—no picture—had ever been sold at auction for more than £31,000. That was a picture by Poussin—the *Adoration of the Magi*—which was sold here and is now in the possession of the National Gallery in London.

'The decision was taken, jointly by us and the vendor, the son of Jacob Goldschmidt, that the sale would be conducted in a different manner from any sales hitherto. The sale would consist of seven pictures only and there would be nothing else sold on that day in the way of pictures—in fact in the way of anything. The gallery was completely empty.

'Secondly—although this doesn't sound very adventurous now, it was the first sale ever to take place at night in Great Britain. We also introduced (I think it was the second time) internal television so that people all over the building—in the basement, God knows where—could watch the sale.

'It was given front-page coverage in the *Daily Express*, on the instructions of Lord Beaverbrook, so that the whole of the country knew about it. Even the taxi driver bringing me to the sale asked me what those pictures were going to fetch that night. It really had captured the imagination of the public.

'At the sale the seven pictures were expected to fetch about £400,000 but actually they fetched £781,000; so that the price of the most expensive picture, one of the two Cézannes which fetched £220,000, was seven times higher than anything had fetched at auction before.

'What it did, of course, was in the first place to transfer attention firmly on the auction front from New York to London. It established that it was possible for people to make up their minds on the spur of the moment to pay these vast sums for a picture or not. Until then it was always believed by dealers, and by a lot of other people who weren't in competition with us, that people would not do that—they would have to have time to think about the money involved and so on.

'How did we come to get the sale? Well, Goldschmidt had had a previous sale here. He came here with his pictures by sea. He didn't have a very good time—he'd been given the wrong forms by a consul's office in New York and when he got to Southampton the Customs wouldn't recognize the forms, and so on. You can imagine he was fairly irascible . . . then he had to choose between us and Christie's and—well he chose us, because his father had had a sale here of Chinese porcelain in the 1930s. Well, we got that sale and had it here and it was a success of sorts. It was a sale of a few Old Masters and other pictures which sold adequately, not wonderfully. But Jacob Goldschmidt was a gambler by nature and by background. He believed in this thing and we tried various combinations in trying to get the sale on the floor. We tried to get someone to guarantee the sale, but that fell through—had they done so they'd have made an unbelievable fortune. And at the same time he had a number of people pressing him to sell privately, but Goldschmidt and his fellow-executor had faith in us and eventually we got the Impressionists to sell without any strings attached at all, and his faith was justified by the results.

'It was a fascinating night. I really felt at the time that there'd never be so much at stake again, and so far, I've been right. When I got to £220,000 for the Cézanne I said "Will *no one* bid any more?" and a great laugh went up. It didn't sound very good at the time. It just slipped out I'm afraid.

'Apart from the Goldschmidt sale, we changed the whole face of the art market in the 'fifties by going over to specialized sales. It was a development of the Goldschmidt idea, I think on the one hand we were prepared to remain very conservative but on the other to become very go-ahead.'

One of his innovations was to hire Drury Lane theatre in which to sell a collection of ballet costumes; and in the middle of the sale to stage a ballet. In fact, if at all possible, Wilson likes to approach a great sale as an artistic presentation in itself.

'Yes, that was quite amusing. We were selling ballet clothes from the Diaghilev era and the costumes from *Sacre de Printemps* which was so revolutionary at the time with music by Stravinsky; and we got dancers from the ballet school to model the costumes and they were going to dance excerpts from the ballet, and we had present someone who had worked under Diaghilev, and I must say the whole thing put me off grants to the young.

'Here was somebody—I mean Diaghilev was a giant in his field—who had been present at the rehearsals of the original production, this monumental break with tradition—the ballet tradition of grace was turned inside out—and while those that were actually taking part in the thing were marvellous everyone else sat around the theatre reading the *Daily Express* and not taking any notice at all. I was amazed.'

Wilson deprecates (but rather likes) the suggestion that he is a swashbuckling businessman who beats the Americans at their own game; but he has no hesitation in describing why he led Sotheby's in their attack on the art market of the United States—an attack which led to Sotheby's acquiring a controlling interest in the Parke–Bernet Galleries and a virtual stranglehold over the American market.

'It's because there's no doubt that America is the great art market of the world', he says and declines to discuss his part (the major role) in a takeover battle which lasted the best part of ten years. But he insists the marriage between Sotheby's and Parke Bernet was for the best for both firms and that all the initial difficulties have been ironed out.

He treats with scorn any suggestion that the art market is crazy; that the huge prices being paid for paintings and objets d'art and so on constitute a bubble which must burst.

'I can prove that's absolute nonsense,' he said. 'The art market's due for a tremendous rise. Allowing for the devaluation of money and choosing only those sections of the market which are fashionable, prices are still remarkably low.

'You can't choose works of art that aren't fashionable—that's not fair. But take Leonardo da Vinci, one of the greatest artists the world has ever known. The Czar, in 1912, bought *The Virgin and Child* by Leonardo for £312,000. That you can multiply by forty to get its value today and that gives you over twelve million pounds. Well, I think a painting was sold privately recently for four million pounds—that's not twelve—and people with four or five millions to spare are a little thin on the ground.

'By comparison, things that were fashionable at the turn of the century were just as expensive then as they are now, if not more so. Contemporary art has always been an excellent investment and I believe strongly that there's going to be a great surge forward in the art market soon. So much more is in museums now which means that there are fewer paintings available for sale—there's a scarcity value on great works of art. If these things were as common as blackberries then obviously they'd fetch much less.'

54. Mr Ivan Chance, Chairman of Christie's from 1958 to 1974.

Mr Chance of Christie's
An Interview

Question: 'Mr Chance. How much of your business is concerned with sentiment; how much with the artistic value of the goods you sell; and how much is the whole thing just money?'

Mr Chance: 'We are, after all, a commercial house. We happen to sell works of art rather than, say, boots and shoes or tobacco—although, come to think of it, we've sold them in our time. But basically, to misquote Cromwell, we know what we're selling and we love what we know. Nobody would be in this business or in this firm if he wasn't passionately interested either in everything he sold or in some specific category. Everyone thinks that we're millionaires ten times over, but this is not true. People tend to see a picture sold for a million pounds and they think "Oh well, Christie's have made a million" but of course we only make the commission (although that's very satisfactory on a million-pound sale). But the overheads are leaping all the time—you can imagine what the rates on this building must be like, the telephone, the post and all that, all that's got to be taken into consideration. If you come into this business, you're going to have a busy life, and exciting life; it's damned hard work but you're not going to make a fortune. It's an abiding pleasure and interest—there's something to be found in the most boring sale.

'Our next duty as a business is to get the maximum price for any article. The more we get for the client the more staisfied the client is, and the more the commission we get for ourselves. And therefore the commercial side inevitably comes in to a large extent. Because of this we, particularly the specialists in a particular line, have to know as far as is humanly possible the approximate market value of all the objects we have sent in for sale. We have to advise the owner of its potential sale value or what reserve to put on.

'Eventually we come to the third thing—somebody has to stand up on a rostrum and sell the articles. That's another side of the business which is extremely interesting—there's the psychological side to it. The longer you're here, the more sales you take, the more you get to understand the idiosyncrasies of human nature. You get to know who bids and how, and basically it's a big battle of wits. They quite naturally are trying to buy as cheaply as possible and we are trying to make them pay as much money as possible. So this is where the skill or science of actually taking a sale comes in.

'Behind all that are the hideously boring administrative problems; dealing with tricky people, dealing with people who—don't we all?—imagine their geese to be swans and who don't take it too kindly when we have to undeceive them. There's always the chap who comes along and tells me that his father always said to him if he got in a mess to bring whatever it is along to me and I'll get a good price for it. It turns out that my own old father sold the goods for his old father, and what we have now is a copy. This happens frequently and I've often felt over the years that I wish to God I could give this old woman a hundred quid—or even the taxi fare home.

'When I came here there were six clerks in the office. Two who did the accounts, two who did the day book and two who did the actual sales. Now I think we have thirty-five. There's a chartered accountant in charge of the accounts department, there are two computers—thirty-five or forty bodies in the accounts department alone—a great number of whom are, of course, acting as unpaid tax collectors for the Government.'

Question: 'Your earliest and most illustrious predecessor was known as the "Specious Orator". There's not much specious oratory about a sale these days—in fact pretty little oratory at all. I was quite disappointed. It's all in the catalogue. Is that a loss?'

Mr Chance: 'I feel it's no more nor less of a loss than the fact that one used to get into a hansom cab and drive to Paddington Station, get a comfortable train with a seat, where you could have a drink brought to you if you wanted one. Like so many good things in life it's gone—gone because it was time-consuming. We now have many more lots on a sale and sell very much quicker than we did when I started. The important picture sales always used to be on a Saturday, starting at one o'clock. There were roughly 120 lots in a sale and the sales lasted about two hours. A lot a minute was the average. Nowadays we reckon to sell—well I do because I'm reckoned to sell pretty fast—a hundred lots an hour. Selling quickly is an art in itself—basically you get people to bid much more quickly because they know if they don't bid they won't get it. It's another part of the technique.'

Question: 'There's obviously a camaraderie between the auction houses and the dealers. Does this lead to the "Rings" we so often read about?'

Mr Chance: 'We can't live without the dealers and they can't live without us. Sometimes there's direct competition between us but more often we act as brokers to the dealers. Because of what we are and because we don't buy outright and therefore don't have to have enormous capital sums available, we can handle and deal with far bigger collections than any dealer conceivably could. There always have been, and because human nature is what it is, there always will be Rings of some sort or another, but at the moment there's nothing of the sort operating in London. Too many people chasing too few goods—you can only have a Ring operating effectively if you've got everyone in it.

'It's a very different affair in the country because there you have the country dealers all knowing each other and the London and overseas dealers simply haven't the time to go to all the country house sales unless there's a specific major sale held by one of the big houses.'

Question: 'As auctioneer, what can you do about a Ring?'

Mr Chance: 'You see the Ring doesn't get away with it by putting on a reserve. But you've got to know your values before you put on your reserve. If you're a country chap who's used to selling sheep and goats and you're suddenly faced with selling a Canaletto then you probably don't know it's a Canaletto, and even if you do you don't know what the value is.

'Anyone in this country who has works of art to sell is mad not to sell them in London—leaving out my firm, if you like. This is the centre—and if you want to sell something, go to the centre. The competition you get here is ten times greater than anywhere in the provinces—Edinburgh, Glasgow, Manchester.'

Question: 'What made Sotheby's and Christie's survive for so long?'

Mr Chance: 'The English *au fond* are a nation of gamblers. Every auction is a form of a gamble. On the one side there are people who reckon they are going to get more than they ask for their goods; on the other people who reckon they're going to get something for less. Secondly, there's integrity—a very important word indeed. Thirdly, there are the commission rates which are the cheapest in the world; and fourthly, the English are still the most conservative nation on earth and they like old-established institutions.'

Question: 'You yourself are a bit of an institution within an institution.'

Mr Chance: 'Well, I've been here a long time.'

Question: 'You must have been liked—really liked I mean—to survive?'

Mr Chance: 'In order not to be pushed out? Right. But seriously, it is a very personal business. This is what I try to get home to all my younger colleagues, that they've got to remember that ultimately the man or the woman or the trustee or whoever it is who comes to sell something at Christie's has got a personal interest in it. They're not selling it because it's no good. They're not selling it for fun. They're selling it for some specific reason and very often it's a wrench for them to part with it. Always—well almost always—the customer is right. And when they're not right we've got to be gentle.'

Index

John, Augustus, 70

Kandinsky, Vassily, 91
Keen, Geraldine, 86–8
Kennedy, Joseph, 35–6
Kennerley, Mitchell, 27–8
Kern, Jerome, 27
Khan, Prince Sadruddin, 62, 63
Kirby, G. T., 24, 25
Kirby, Thomas E., 22–5, 26, 30
Knoedler, 23
Koetzer, Leonard, 47, 49
Kraus, H. P., 43

Landrigen, Edward J., 103
Landsdowne, Lord, 18
Landseer, Charles, 17
Lankrink, 59
Le Brun, Vigée, 9
Lecadre, Dr and Mme, 69
Leggatt, Hugh, 88
Leigh, George, 4, 5
Lemoyne, Jean Baptiste, 80
Le Noir, Etienne, 109
Lindsay, the Hon. Patrick, 87
Logan, Milton, 27–8
Lorenzoni, Michele, 99
Lorraine, Claude, 106
Lurcy, Georges, 29

Manet, Edouard, 42–5
Marc, Franz, 91
Marie-Feodorovna, Grand Duchess, 84
Marion, Louis, 29
Massey, Raymond, 103
Maugham, Somerset, 52–3
McKay, Andrew, 13
Millais, Sir John Everett, 17
Millar, Oliver, 59
Mitchell, Milton, 27
Modigliani, Amédéo, 74–5
Monet, Claude, 65, 68–9
Moore, Henry, 91–2
Moore, Rufus E., 22
Morgan, Charles, 22
Morgan, Mary Jane, 22
Morgan, John Pierpont, 27, 43

Mostyn-Owen, William, 87, 107
Mountain, Sir Brian and Sir Edward, 30
Müller, William James, 17

National Gallery (British), 89, 90
Nelson, Admiral Lord, 9–10, 86
Newlands, Lord, 14
Nixon, Edith, 27

Palmer, Samuel, 106
Palomino, Antonio, 85
Parke, Major Hiram T., 25–9
Partridge, Frank, 57
Pascin, Jules, 75
Pevsner, Anton, 92
Philip, King of Spain, 89
Picasso, Pablo, 55–6
Pigot, George, 93
Pissarro, Camille, 54, 56
Pitcairn, the Rev, Thomas, 65, 68–9
Porter, Endymion, 60
Poussin, Nicholas, 111

Quaritch, Bernard, 24

Radcliffe, Sir Everard, 1, 4
Rembrandt, Harmenszoon van Rijn (Ryn), 18, 25–6, 30–2, 71–2
Renoir, Pierre Auguste, 29, 46, 75, 92
Renwick, William Goodwin, 99
Reynolds, Debbie, 103
Reynolds, Sir Joshua, 8, 17
Ribouleau, Isaac, 105
Roseberry, Lord, 18
Rose Terrace, 78–9, 80–1
Rosin, Bert, 103
Rouault, Georges, 73
Rousseau, Henri, 91
Rovensky, Mrs Sarah, 29
Rubens, Peter Paul, 47, 58–61

Sabet, H., 84
Sakomoto, Mr, 96
Sargent, John Singer, 14, 20–1
Savage, Robert, 59–61
Shirley Temple's Teddy bear, 103

Simon, Norton, 71–2, 92
Simpson, Colin, 87
Sisley, Alfred, 52, 56
Smit, Philippe, 68
Somerset, David, 71, 72
Sotheby, John, 5
Sparks, John, 96
Speelman, Edward, 30
Stradivari, Antonio, 100–1
Stubbs, George, 93–5
Sutton, Richard F., 22
Swann, Arthur, 24

Taylor, Basil, 93–5
Taylor, Elizabeth, 92
Tennant, Margaret, 18
Titian, Tiziano Vecellio, 85, 89–90
Toulouse-Lautrec, 53
Turner, Emery S., 24
Turner, Joseph, 23

Van Dyck, Sir Anthony, 18, 90
Vandegrift, Mary, 29
Van Gogh, Vincent, 18, 42, 65–8, 92
Van Risenburgh, Bernard, 84
Velasquez, Diego Rodriguez de Silva y, 21, 85, 86, 87, 88
Victoria, Princess, 16
von Thyssen, Baron, 62, 63
Vuillaume, J. P., 100–1

Warre, Felix, 5
Weitzner, Julius, 89–90
Wernher, Lady, 14, 15–16
Westminster, Duke of, 49
Wilde, Cornel, 103
Wildenstein, Alec, 88
Wilkinson, John, 5
Williamson, Dr Peter, 33
Wilson, Peter, 32, 95, 110–13
Wilson, President Woodrow, 14
Winston, Harry, 63
Winters, David, 103
Wood, Natalie, 103
Woodward, Joanne, 103

Yerkes, Charles T., 23
Yerkes sale, 23–4